SHARE
SUSTAIN
SURVIVE

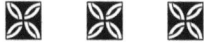

GARY DALEN

Side Effects Press

→→ →→→→→→←

Side Effects Press

→→→→→←

PO BOX 12232
Westminster CA
92685
www.sideeffects.com

share sustain survive

Printed in the United States
ISBN 978-0-578-01200-1

(Johnny boy)

Have you seen hope & love winding down the avenue?
In the alley of despair where dark clouds gather around,
Johnny boy what have you done to be lying down in the
city of doom, on the wrong side of an angry moon
loneliness can be so cruel.
Won't you join me in a drink or two so we can salute the
blues.

Can't you see that he's got to be real that he can't hide
anything inside.
So he'll see you in the morning time, he'll see you in the
sunrise.

He's a lonely man rubbing his eyes drinking love from an
empty cup.
He's afraid of the love he don't feel he just can't seem to
follow his will.
He don't want to live he don't want to die he just wants to
lay down and cry.
He can't run he can't hide I always knew that he wouldn't
survive.

Can't you see that he's got to be real that he can't hide anything inside.
So he'll see you the morning time, he'll see you in the sunrise.

He would always hope that you would transcend above the foolishness of this land.
Every night and every day he would sit alone and watch the parade go by, it never seemed to want to change its song it seemed satisfied to only belong,
When will these thoughts stop pounding his head can only wear relief in the dead.

Can't you see that he's got to be real that he can't hide anything inside.
So he'll see you in the morning time he'll see you in the sunrise.

Contents

(The Johnny Crawford diaries)

$ins & Nonsense

Creation is a miracle with unlimited possibilities. Our bodies could have been created any number of ways whatever the creator's intention. For some reason the creator designed our physical bodies to require food and water. I think it's interesting as to why we were designed in this particular way. I mean we could have just as easily been designed as to where our bodies didn't require food and water in order to survive. For example I would assume just as easily our bodies could have been made to where we only needed to breathe the air and /or perhaps receive some form of nutrition from the sun in order to survive. So why did the creator design us to need food and water? Could it of possibly been just to see how we would co-exist with each other on a planet with a finite supply of food and water? To see how we would organize and distribute the food and water? In other words how would we evolve as a human species under these particular circumstances? Would we share the food and water equally as well as conserve and protect the needed resources or would we separate and divide into different groups or nations and fight for more than what we need without having any thought to conservation and environmental protection? Is all this just possibly some plan and/or experiment to see how humanity plays out its evolutionary role, determining if will come together and survive or separate and dissolve?

I don't know exactly what it is but when I am walking or driving around town and I observe people engaged in their work, whatever it may be, I can't help but feel something is wrong with this picture, that something just isn't right, something is missing. There is this feeling deep down in my gut that the type of work people are doing is inherently wrong, that it is not a natural act and people are just mislead to believe things could not possibly be any other way. It is what people refer to as the real world, working in order to survive. But I think it is a big lie it really doesn't have to be this way there must be alternative ways for society to survive and/or thrive that would be much more pleasing and fulfilling for the individual than the demeaning, boring, drudgery of labor. Yea I walk around town and all I see is people working at boring jobs and buying boring things, the survival of nothing. But as academia is coming to realize there is not one absolute reality but many observer created realties so the reality of work can be uncreated as easily as it was created. All belief systems can change.

I thought I had heard Dostoevsky say something like the world could only be saved by beauty. Who are the visionaries, artists, entrepreneurs, corporate developers, architects, white and blue collar workers that created the run down trashy suburbs and all the strip malls, Fast food joints like Burger king, McDonalds, KFC, Subway, gas stations, 7-11's, auto mechanic shops, gun shops, check cashing stores, wall marts, k marts, it's all crap. The streets all cluttered with garbage, all those rundown buildings, sixties style architecture needing paint and repair, abandoned buildings businesses gone bad. Abandoned buildings probably owned by some rich real estate profiteer holding on to them waiting for the market to change using them in the mean time as a tax right off. There are thousands & thousands of abandoned buildings and thousands & thousands of homeless people, go figure.

I hate those 6 lane wide suburban boulevards where people drive their polluting internal combustion SUV's as fast as they can, racing past strip malls displaying legalized neon corporate graffiti, trying to beat the red light. What I really get angered by is the shiny new BMW's weaving in and out of traffic, I mean that is dangerous it could cause an accident and kill an innocent child. But I rarely see them get tickets because they are what the status quo wants, not people tripping on acid and brainstorming radical new ideas for a more fulfilling society.

Street artists in any given town see how a sick cult of anti-aesthetic commerce turns their neighborhoods into such garbage dumps therefore proceed to act out by covering the town with illegal art. They are fighting fire with fire, the fire of mass media. Mass media is the most powerful weapon to ever ascend upon the planet for it has the means to control the masses. People are social beings susceptible to peer pressure, they want to be accepted and they do this by acting normal. And what is considered to be the norm is always defined by the mass media under the manipulative direction of the corpotocracy, the illuminated elite. Only about two percent of the population is immune from the mass media so therefore have the responsibility of pushing and pulling human evolution onward.

Yea it's all about political aesthetics. Some want just parts of the world beautiful for a select few who live in guarded, gated, communities and vacation at private resorts, with huge walls separating and protecting them from the poor local folks. But for the few humans who have not yet been corrupted by society's false promises of riches want the whole world beautiful with more natural landscapes, indiscriminate cooperative communities that are inspiring to all. Awe, the aesthetic appeal of a natural healthy environment, clean water, clear blue sky and sweet tasting soil, to be able to joyfully acquire the basic needs for survival and have the opportunity to spend a lot of time with friends and family, engaging in art and personal contemplative reflection; where everyone has the opportunity to realize their fullest creative potential by cultivating their intrinsic individual personalities. A society of openness and acceptance, unity within diversity, a world of few laws if no laws at all but only self organizing pragmatic collective communities dynamically unfolding out of an un-imposed natural experience.

I don't like poverty it's ugly. I don't like living on infested streets with hopeless drug abuse, gang violence, domestic violence, trash everywhere, crime, the sounds of sirens, broken down buildings, bars on the windows, torn screens, abandoned buildings, money marts, fast food chains, I am describing a fairly good portion of the world, the face of depression. We have created through our collective consciousness a vast wasteland of horrific human starvation. Who can see beauty in that, anyone? This happens because we are misinformed unable to see over the wall, overtaking by fear and greed, hoarding more than what we need, lacking awareness and retrospection. We need to be connecting with each other at a deeper level beyond the hypocritical sentimentalism of religion, engaging into more satisfying experiences of sexual pleasure, music, dancing in solidarity, drinking homemade wine, always creating alternate modes of entertainment and pleasure.

I don't know maybe the problem is parental teaching. We have not yet evolved enough as a society to have the right, the ability, or the wisdom to teach our children about love, justice, sharing and peace. Maybe we need to reverse the process and have the children teach us. But I doubt that will ever come to pass, so if we are to continue to teach our children then let us not teach them the morality of right and wrong but teach them the equilibrium of justice, the inner roots of love, compassion and selflessness and then perhaps the morality of doing the right thing will naturally fall into place and not from being obedient to the institutions of church and state. {Jesus said: The old man will not hesitate to ask a seven day old baby about the place of life, and he will live.}

The bottom line is many parts of the world are ugly, cities, towns, villages, communities; whole nations infested with poverty and environmental pollution, war and crime everywhere, just outright misery. The people who are poor say this ugliness is caused by an unequal distribution of capital and this inequality causes poverty and in turn this poverty causes crime, dissent, violence, riots and social unrest leading to revolution. Rich People go to Wars >Poor People go to Revolutions.

So next time the peace-niks are out in the streets protesting against the status quo and all their wars with their bull horn chants I will thank them and wish them well. Who knows maybe someday I will get enough courage to join them in the streets hand in hand, because I do so dearly want the world to be beautiful. A lot of people don't like the protesters. Pop culture and the media are always making fun of them. Every time they are portrayed on TV sitcoms they make them out to look like obnoxious idiots. Why is that? Are they a threat to someone? Maybe they even get on my nerves at times with their bull horn chanting, as I mumble to myself "dam why don't they just let it go and chill out" but just think how fucked up the world might be if they weren't out there day in and day out demonstrating, screaming out there slogans, protesting against the powers to be and all its propaganda. I mean the world would be an all around ugly ghetto out of complete control and beyond repair if they weren't out there protesting against all the daily corporate pollution and greed. And when you break it all down all their doing is protesting against the unequal distribution of wealth and its negative side effects causing the de-beautification of the natural world, the breeding of the of anti-aesthetics cult. Maybe this is what Dostoevsky meant by the world can only be saved by beauty.

—

My name is Johnny Crawford and I am not feeling very good today, my whole body creaks and crawls, no sign of relief. It feels feverish and shaky. I can't deal with anybody any more, human contact is painful, making me desperately lonely, especially for a women. Nobody wants me and I don't want anybody, at least at this peculiar moment in reality. My whole mouth hurts, my teeth are rotting out. I've got this swollen bump in my lower right gum. It scares me. I wonder what it is, it could be serious and very expensive to fix. I don't have any money at all right now; I can barely afford to eat. What am I going to do? I can't handle it. I'm falling apart I'm terrified. Oh spirit where are you come and enter my fragile being and deliver me just as you did Saint John of the Cross and all the enlightened people who have inhabited this planet in their physical bodies but somehow managed to have their minds carried away to a supernatural state of spiritual ecstasy. But not I, hell I can't even drink anymore for I've been informed by the healthcare experts to stop enjoying the wine. My body is tumbling, spiraling in the abyss of alienation, alone in hell, experiencing the pure existence of inverted orgasms. I can't move my body it's shackled to the couch that comforts my aching soul. Its purpose serves me. I'm abandoned. I shall pray for a guardian angel disguised as a beautiful sexy model just like the one on the cover of glamour magazine that lies still on the table staring at me, teasing me to tears. How wonderful, how joyful it would be if she knocked on my door right now. She would come in and sit down on the couch right next to me. The couch would come alive in spirit. I would smile; my blood would flow as if cabernet were running through me. Oh, the scent of her flesh, the vision of her smile, the sound of her voice, the movement of her aura healing all my pain. My body would open up and move all my cells would tingle in celebration. I would be happy; I would have the genuine confidence of a winner. She would smile at me and say my name, awe such a sweet sounding name. Rub her hands through my hair. I then would be delivered, breaking through the shackles that incarcerate me. I would be able to walk out the front door with my head held up high wearing that big grin of confidence. I would confront everybody with hugs and smiles. I could take on the whole world and save it from self-destruction. I would become the most famous leader the world has ever known.

But no she has not come and she never will. I truly and honestly believe she will never come. I'm completely hopeless. I don't believe in miracles. All I can do is numb my mind and gaze out the window into the dull, boring, dead gray afternoon sky. Bending over I put my head down in despair covering my feverish face with my vulnerable human hands, thinking, wondering and dreaming. Oh where did I go wrong? I have failed the American dream. I'm a middle-aged loser. I have no money, no talents, no friends, no country and very little mother earth.

I'm afraid if I completely snap and go insane I won't be able to protect myself from invisible demons disguised as my countrymen. Should I go to the mental institution? I doubt I would ever have the strength or the money to take on such an adventure. Or maybe I would be better off going to the monastery. Perhaps there I may come unto kind, sensitive, warm-hearted spirits that would permeate through the pores of my infected soul and deliver me inside to love. The spirits at the mental institution might corrupt me, strangle me and brutalize my sensitive ego. That sounds terrifying to be controlled in a place with florescent lighting, solid core metal doors, semi modern furniture that reaps of societal control, masses victimized by culture, the social norm of insanity. A place where dark stained plastic molding blares out against white colored sheet rocked walls. Walls displaying boring, sentimental, mushy paintings that were probably purchased at wall mart, showing no signs of life, giving witness to the subtle realities ensnared behind the walls of this place, the walls of towns, the walls of states, the walls of nations, the walls of the world, the walls of the universe, the walls of my minds predicament. But one good thing about the mental institution is I might find a woman there who might be a tormented nut like me. We could fall in love and after treatment get married, go on a honeymoon to Disneyland and go shopping together. We could also have children who we would properly train and condition so that they could easily adapt to the status quo and therefore not suffer as we have.

Most people in this country deep down are just as depressed as I am, some probably more, some less, but nonetheless people are depressed. Any person with even a minor degree of sensitivity could not help but feel depressed in such a cruel, unjust, violent world. A lot of them won't admit they are depressed because they are in denial. They just can't except that life is hell so they try to pretend to themselves they are happy; plus they don't want to be seen as being depressed because in most circles of society it is not socially acceptable; its taboo. And of course everyone wants to be accepted by their social peers for as Berger says we are a social something.

I believe one of the main reasons people are so depressed is because they either don't have a job or they are over worked at a job they don't like. Usually the main motivation to work beyond basic survival is the desire for nonessential stuff. But a lot of people who make a lot of money from their job are so stressed out and over worked they can't even enjoy the financial rewards received from their ambitious hustling. The US has the highest rate of mental illness, a byproduct of living in a dysfunctional economy of trickledown economics and over consumption of cheap made junk. Generally speaking for most people work sucks, everyone is competing for that promotion and raise. Usually the person with the greatest success, the over achiever with an ingrained, arrogant over load of self-confidence (Dale Carnegie gone mad) is the one who wins. A free market monetary system is designed on the concept of competition, thus competition becomes necessary for human survival, inevitably causing one to love money and wisdom has revealed before our very eyes that the love for money is the root of all evil.

It's all about making money in order to create the illusion of success, a side effect of influential peer pressure. If you don't work or want luxury and material wealth society demonizes and stigmatizes you as a mad man and nobody wants that. If someone were to truly act like Jesus they would probably become ostracized from family and friends for acting irrational and appearing to eccentric. If you are not accepted in the worldly plane what can you do? Do you change your ways so you can be accepted? Or do you try and transcend beyond the need for acceptance into the blue light knowing that the worldly plane is not authentic acceptance and love but only an illusion? I believe the underlying desire for material success is not for the substance of the material but for the desire to be loved, or perhaps to suppress the pain of not being loved for who you really are. I think Thomas Merton said, "Often our need for others is not love at all but only the need to be sustained in our illusions even as we sustain others in theirs."

In order to acquire material abundance you must work harder and more efficient than the next guy always staying focused and loyal to the American, Corporate, Christian work ethic. And as an extra added advantage in the quest for material success most people will pray to their god or chant some new age mantra. There are multitudes of books written on the spiritual path to wealth and abundance. The people who buy these books probably already have more money than half of the world's people, what a joke, what a spiritual crisis.

So whether you have a job or not you will probably be depressed you just won't realize it though because you have become distracted by the graces of the American Dream. But you will probably be more depressed if you don't have a job, although you would probably be able to function more genuinely from an inner space as you would become isolated, alienated, a social outcast cast out of the American social club for not paying your dues. For nobody wants to associate with you because they fear the thought of not having a job and you will remind them of that fear. There will be much gossip behind your back. So they don't want to be in your presence because it makes it more difficult for them to stay in that space of denial, which is perfectly understandable.

I haven't worked in eight weeks. That's OK by me, but I am getting stressed out about making rent. I work for myself because I have a phobia of bosses. I fear they might yell at me. I guess I feel this way because of my lack of self-confidence and my intense sensitivity to negative feedback. I have always been exploited by every boss I've had they never paid me what I am truly worth. Most bosses I had worked for were assholes, which is why I got fed up and begun to work on my own. I became my own boss and paid myself fairly for what I was really worth. But I just can't get enough work because I'm not good at smoozing, networking, marketing, selling myself. And I don't have a lot of contacts, acquaintances, or friends. Actually I don't have any friends being too sensitive for human interaction. So I guess this lack of competitive self-confidence cuts down on my ability to conjure up steady work. But that's OK I don't want steady work anyway; I just need enough money to pay rent, eat, and maybe get a sensual massage on a good month.

Eighty percent of the time I am in a state of chaos, spiritually, morally and socially confused, a complete neurotic nut case, stressed out and uptight. Ten percent of the time I am bestowed upon by divine grace where I can feel a fleeting moment of relief, a feeling of lightness, floating in peace. Yes in spite of my neurosis I am still connected to the graces of eternal peace and joy, I just lack the realization most of the time of what I truly am; I am love and will always be loved no matter what from here through eternity. No matter how much of an asshole I am, a no good for nothing lazy loser I will always be loved. For all my thoughts and fears are only an illusion I experience when I am not in state of grace. Everything else I do, think, or say when not I am not in a state of grace is only for the purpose of self-indulging entertainment and of course for the reason of escape through distraction.

It takes a lot of hard work and courage to satisfy the ego. It is very difficult to live up to the mask of identity. It is just a pain in the ass to have to constantly satisfy your ego. My ego causes me much suffering because its desires are never fulfilled. I deeply desire to rise above mediocrity but I have failed every attempt therefore I wallow in deep depression. I am a failed artist unable to submit to convention. Living in mediocrity terrifies me but I don't have the courage, genius, brilliance, intelligence, talent, skill, or discipline to rise above it, I would rather sleep. In order to attract a beautiful, sexy, women I can't just be a painter I have to be an art star. I want to be famous but I live a non-existent life with no friends or lovers. I want to destroy my ego because it would end all the pain of failure, a deeply intensified pain. My ego is deflated but fully alive, noxiously immortal. Yes my severe depression makes me lazy lacking the structure and discipline to obtain my goals. I spend my time lying on the couch just dreaming about it and drink spirits to numb the pain of no success but only loneliness, rejection, alienation, disappointment. I think Van Gogh once asked, when would that colony of artist be founded, where the poor cab horses of painting could find a warm refuge, and be protected from the harshness of life? I can relate.

People find their identity through creation by what they create. If there is no depth to their creation there is no depth to their identity. And by having a lack of identity one feels alienated from others. Ultimately what one wants to create are ways to experience deeper connection and unity with others. A society that either directly or indirectly suppresses genuine creativity ultimately creates a society of alienation. There becomes an imbalance of power expelling more energy for mechanical production and less energy for authentic self-realization, leading to false identity through fear.

When we have a thought it instantaneously connects with everything, everything being tangled up as one. All causes and effects are just temporal illusions through experiencing reality stuck between the confines of a time-space continuum for reasons beyond thought. The ego is our teacher through the experiences we all encounter in the universal relativity of a mutual arising, within a connected network we are taught that we don't need the ego because it is an illusion, just as we come to know cause and effect is nothing more than a misunderstood illusion, having no real meaning within and beyond space and time. When we become fully aware of whom we truly are, no one, we don't need the ego teacher anymore. So our ego is not our enemy but only our teacher, are only teacher, all the others are false prophets and charlatans. So after we learn by experiencing the lessons of the illusive sin that cause can have effect and realize that there is no such thing as cause and affect but only an infinite pool of mutual oneness we then no longer need our teacher.

The ego serves a divine purpose so don't ever try to escape or destroy your ego, you embrace it in order to learn from it, eventually evolving beyond its divisionary nature, the labyrinth. If ultimate reality is beyond space-time causality then ultimate happiness is beyond space-time causality. So don't become detached from life but fully embrace it. Become attached to your desires, dreams, emotions, fantasies, thoughts, senses and flesh. We are here to experience life so fully embrace what is now. But one thing for sure when it comes to sensual indulgence you should be cautioned against material accumulation for the planet will not survive if one person has more that they need. We must live in ecological economics. Share Sustain Survive

Life is the process of surrendering to mystery in all its passionate, terrifying beauty. In living you surrender your consciousness to mystery enabling you to unfold, evolving as a dynamic, creative, unique but universally interconnected adolescent essence, expanding beyond fixed illusions and linguistic symbols of ignorance into a space of absolute truth where a single life moment possess six billion realities. The universe is consciousness realized in so as consciousness is the universe expanding as one through the illusive karmic process of the illusive nature of cause and effect revealing reincarnation as a meaningless concept just as are boundaries of time and space. There is no concrete core of independent intrinsic reality to any being or anything reality is only to be found through the interaction of all that is. This therefore would justify the equal sharing of the earth's bread in the process of satisfying our divine appetites, the nourishment of souls.

—

Yes work has always been a struggle for me rooted in my lack of confidence to perform the duties that are required of me in order to get paid. I tremble in fear that I should not be able to perform adequately and therefore get reprimanded and scolded for my incompetence; it is without a doubt a deeply embedded phobia. It takes a lot of confidence to survive in a capitalist society. The competition is unbearable, causing enormous stress and anxiety leading me into the confines of inescapable fear where I am daily fed doses of loveless depression.

My soul is very sensitive and fragile. Inspiration oh inspiration where art thou? I have nothing left but bills. I owe God lots of money, Loans, loans, loans but no work that pays and pays twenty dollars an hour. Yes at twenty dollars an hour I could pay God back. I could leap out of the class of slave labor. Yes, at twenty dollars an hour I would be making a lot especially if I was working forty hours a week. I might even acquire a Christian work ethic. Work hard at being a hard worker, a man respected by the community; a man of great virtue and righteousness: a hard working responsible god fearing man, the good old work ethic. Yes at twenty dollars an hour I could be very productive so productive I could buy a nice car and then attract a woman, only a plain woman I suppose no super models of course. But heck, at least I could probably get some woman to marry me if I were making twenty dollars an hour. My labor would be productive, making everyone happy and proud of me, especially the boss man who pays me twenty dollars an hour. What a generous good Christian he is for paying me twenty an hour, which is a lot of money, he must be very well off.

Everybody is stressed out about competing for that twenty-dollar an hour job. And if they get it they are still under a lot of stress to keep up the pace of productivity in order to maintain the twenty-dollar an hour job. You can't escape the stress whether on the top or the bottom. Stress causes drug and alcohol abuse, divorce, endless supply of anti-depressants, domestic violence, crime, suicide, disease, cancer, heart attacks, mental illness, over weight dysfunctional children, and ultimately war between nations. But as conventional wisdom has it that just the way the world is, it's not supposed to be fair. That's not true, but even if it were true it doesn't have to stay that way because after all science does say the nature of the universe is change, self organizing, co-evolving, so anything is possible in a creative dynamic universe.

We are creative organisms perhaps unable to control but we can create change. Controlling is an anomaly to change and creativity. And creativity and change are synonymous so controlling in essence is suppressing creative evolution. So now let's relate this back to the economics of survival and the twenty dollars an hour job. In other words I don't need to control the system I just need to change the economic structure so it's not so stressful, acting out as a self-organizing creative organism. We breathe to create, to evolve, to survive not to make twenty dollars an hour. Our nature is survival. So we create in order to change the environment to a space that's less stressful, making our experience on earth more pleasurable.

Life for sure is a paradox; everything is true as well as false. Everything is good as well as evil. Even though life sucks it is Holy. My confidence is low. I feel less than good, less than God. My poor health doesn't help either. I am the situated spectacle of anguish and suffering offering up platitudes of life's meaning. Joys emerge sometimes out of astrological luck, superstitious wishing, postmodern self-help, spiritual sideshows and brain washing, but never enough for its mostly suffering. Is my suffering self inflicted or institutionally caused through patterns of strange attractors causing effects, karma, karma, dharma, dharma, blown to bits. Thy kingdom come thy will be done on earth as it is in heaven give us this day our daily bread and twenty dollars an hour and an automobile that goes real fast. Breathing power, injecting fuel, excreting demons both red white and blue; exercising anger in the constant frustrations of unrequited lust, being disconnected always and forever. It seems that the root cause of fear leads to the mysteries of death, the unknown ultimate orgasm, as we sit, watch and wait, masturbating purposely.

Negative awareness, is suffering self inflicted or being institutionally shot at us through the political will, the internal combustion engine of laissez faire economics? Antidotes of postmodern paraquat inhalation, spiritual naturalness, ego beyond ego, no ego, all ego, Gods ego, ego orgasm, the free will to feel the self, to touch the self, to hold the self, to love the self; the aesthetics of self mutilation, eastern performance art, guru worship, lingam worship, yoni worship, the mechanics of body athletics, God is a performance artist, obviously.

Was past tense 'now', according to relativity it has no escape. Forget it. No escape. The future is an illusion. The past of course is only ego excretion. The Buddha spirit has finally become conscious of itself, self realized in the context of no self, no soul. It's only the coming awareness of Sangha. Yes the Dali lama is fed up as well as Thich Nhat Hanh and god dammit I am fed up to. Yes it's true we are a self-evolving cooperative organism. It's true the untouchables are tired of not being touched. We have evolved from the desire to have no desire, from the practice of rituals, which brings the promise of personal spiritual liberation that transcends the material, psychological, social confines of the world, a state of peace devoid of passion and attachment. We have been liberated from the state of surrendering to worldly incarceration, (Lavkodaya) "mundane awakening," objectives achieved and recognized in this lifetime.

Other worldly enlightenment must be balanced with worldly enlightenment, the middle way. You can't have one without the other, the yin/yang concept. You must meet "basic human needs" in order to achieve supernatural enlightenment, such as a clean and beautiful environment, an adequate supply of safe drinking water, self-created art clothing, balanced nutritious diet, simple but aesthetic housing, holistic healing and energy, communication, education related to life and living and free access to pornography and philosophy books.

Another basic need I forgot to mention is the need to go shopping. I mean that seems to be a great need for the human species. The need to shop, consume, buy, collect, acquire and purchase the material product, the iconography of planet earth. It's almost like planet earth is nothing more than a shopping mall in the greater cosmos. Humans are purchasers who love to shop and buy. It's an obsession, a spiritual ritual. Everything becomes a capital commodity from toothpaste to political candidates, shop, shop, shop until you drop the cultural lyrics of capitalism. This is why capitalism will always flourish because capitalism and shopping are synonymous.

The problem with this iconographical addictive obsession with shopping is there our limited funds and products to go around. So life on earth becomes a fight, gang warfare at the bottom Hiroshima explosions at the top for the means to currency, purchasing power, the acquisition of money so you can buy the symbols of success. Products become an institutionalized deity. The wave of capitalism spreads like a pandemic throughout the world bringing along with it the side effects of greed, crime, addiction, war, poverty, injustice, intolerance, incarceration and racism, the whole nine yards. I mean the world is going to be a continual state of war and social unrest as long as everybody is craving to go shopping.

Let me make myself clear! Only until everybody becomes poor will there be no more poor. Yes problems do arise when just a little under half of the world's people, 3 billion, are surviving on just a few dollars a day, 1.4 billion actually live on less than $1.25 a day. And only 20% of the world's population, US & Europe, account for 60% of the world's consumer spending. So stats like these in a world of shoppers, purchasers and buyers can only guarantee continual stress in all its various shapes, forms and social functions. Ideas from ancient pali scriptures (suttas) "allude that crime and immorality in society are rooted in poverty, (cakkauatti-sihanada-sutta) and that employment opportunities ensure the common weal" (Kutadanta-Sutta)

I don't know maybe my observations on shopping are wrong. I know there are things I most certainly like to purchase. But nonetheless I see commodity shopping as an addiction to a material illusion, psychological manipulation, not a basic need. The objective is to control democratic minds through corporate consumerism while at the same time creating enormous wealth at the top. Maybe we should replace product malls with sex malls by breaking down the chain of sexual repression, where people go and engage in sex, (I'm not talking about prostitution here), but where people go and engage in sex free of charge, an inclusive, sacred, sensual community experience. Sexuality is a not physical pleasure but more of a spiritual unity of pleasure. The degree of pleasure one feels in sex is more dependent on a state of spiritual union and having little to do with bodily functions, or to be fair it's actually more of a body-mind-soul connection resulting in spiritual ecstasy via orgasm. The sharing of sexual love is a key element in learning unconditional love, forgiveness and the self-realization of our interdependence. Human interaction, sensual touch, I don't know it all sounds pretty scary to me. I mean people our disgusting why would you want to touch them, it might be easier to go to war and shoot at them, that's probably why in our culture violence and war are more acceptable forms of expression than sexuality.

—

I have no freedom because I lack certain skills of personality. So I can't work where I want. I can't purchase what I want. I can't wear what I want. I can't drive what I want. I can't travel where I want. I can't eat what I want. I can't live where I want. Plus I am not allowed to smoke in my rented apartment or invite my relatives to stay with me or even have a dog. No freedom. Liberation, Oh liberation, where art thou thy founding fathers of liberty. It's all about the personality and the powers of the zodiac. Oh dear Jesus liberate all my brothers and sisters from violence, injustice, oppression, immoral degradation, and toxic poverty so I can die a white man in peace. For my white blood has had many marks against its tone and mannerisms of misconduct in the context of playing homage to the deities of deception, the cosmology of "Survival of the Fittest" Spencer's curiosity of a dog eat dog brotherhood, cheek to cheek, back to front.

It seems like compassion lies at the root of social activism. Compassion is I suppose to feel empathy for others. To empathize what it would be like to be in their shoes (maybe they can't afford shoes). Thinking that if I were suffering I would hope someone would want to help me. Say for instance if I were oppressed I would hope someone might feel compelled out of empathy to actively help to liberate me from my oppressors, or from toxic poverty, or incarceration for getting caught in the act of surviving off the crumbs of political science.

Charity serves two main purposes usually rooted within a religious context there by relieving the rich of guilt and giving hope to the poor that upon giving they will receive more in return. True charity comes as social transformation. Human rights worker Kevin Danaher said "Instead of asking the charity question, how do we feed all the hungry people? We should ask the solidarity question, "What changes do we need to make in the structures of economics and political power so that everyone can feed themselves?" Genius.

Is it a divine collective calling as a human species to actively participate in the eradication of social injustice, inequality and suffering, to collectively evolve towards world peace moment to moment, to co-create the initial works of god almighty? The dynamic self-organizing organisms we are, adjusting, evolving, co-creating for the whole and not the individual but as an individualized cooperative competing for the whole.

You can't have inner peace without first having world peace. Before we can begin to find peace within ourselves we must first change our collective social structure to a space that effortlessly cultivates universal peace and then and only then can we begin to find peace within ourselves because only then will we have the space to actualize it and finally come to know the inner peace that has been patiently waiting our arrival.

The dark night of the soul, I question its role its purpose. It serves me not, no light, no light, all I can see is no light. The world need not suffer in darkness in order to surrender soul unto light. This concept of trials and tribulations as a necessary process in the path to find god is suspect. It is just another excuse for suffering, suffering caused by greed, exploitation and ignorance. No it need not, it only need to turn on the light of free will, utilize the choice, the choice to smile, play, be happy instead of surrendering to ignorance and a life of meaningless work/jobs for the sake of illusive survival. We will eventually as light overcome ignorance creating an environment for our free will to blossom reaching higher levels of freedom and creation never before imagined.

You want a work ethic I'll give you a work ethic. Work, work, your divine ass off, labor, labor your soul. But do it by choice, do it by liberation, in liberation and through liberation, working for peace, social justice, economic equality and people-hood. Don't work for the "boss man"; please don't work for the boss man, the dictator of commerce, spectacle of Christian gold, the capitol will of money making money exploiting fundamental slave sisters and children of war. We survive off affection and strokes of attention through the means of free market capitalism. We don't get much though so life is suffering and disappointment. But still we hold on to the capital will, we cherish it, we cling to it through all the toxic pain, hoping for fame, more or less an abusive mark on the face of God, if even that. That is why when people are asked why they're against the war they say because it costing too much money, never because it's bloody murder.

There needs to be an equal distribution of the earth's resources for no one has the right to have more than the other. I don't think the earth is equally distributing the food and if it is not happening, why not? Could it be that the human species is not intelligent enough, or spiritually evolved enough to share equally? Are our brains malfunctioning, they say we only use five percent? Are we nothing more or less than savages, greedy selfish pigs? Is that all there is to it? We are just not spiritually, intellectually evolved enough. But we go to our churches don't we? For example the Christian church worships the god Jesus and Jesus teaches us to share the planets resources but do we listen to him, it seems not so. And if someone does listen to him and speaks out about sharing the natural resources they get labeled as being unpatriotic or a communist and sometimes even have to go to jail for speaking out on behalf of his saviors policies of sharing. For example the people who went to jail in the WTO protests. Martin Luther King went to jail. I guess you could say the true teachings of Jesus are a threat to national security. A lot of folks will tell you differently though by turning the scriptures around to justify inequality and war. The bottom line is people can believe anything they want. But we can probably see eye to eye on one thing and that is we all know it is an immoral, narcissistic, savage, greedy, uncultivated, benighted habitat we have created for ourselves. It seems pretty obvious just by smelling and looking around.

According to science we are an interdependent, self-organizing, dynamic system evolving for the betterment of the whole. So the concept of individual enlightenment is really a meaningless concept since we are all interconnected as brothers and sisters. So that is why traditional Buddhism has begun changing in some circles to a more socially collectively engaging space of enlightenment that is being brought forth through the socially mindful teachings of the Dali Lama, Thich Nhat Hanh, among others, as well as the Christian liberation theology of the late assassinated archbishop Oscar Romero. The universe is in a constant state of flux so why should spiritual consciousness remain static or usual.

Tell me can you with a full stomach look directly into the eye of someone who is hungry and say to them that is just the way it is, that we cannot change things so just except your hunger? There can be no purpose in a world of 'It's not supposed to be fair, it's just the way it is.' If this is true then why bother to give charity, or vote, or organize a means to end human suffering among people who are poor and oppressed, why bother to be creative or do anything at all. Why bother to have any form of organized political institutions at all just let money reign. I am not a benevolent all loving person but a selfish person looking out for myself but I still want freedom, justice and equality for all for that will make for a more harmonious, aesthetically pleasing world which will make me happier and I want to be happy, feel more relaxed, feel safe.

Although the current political institutions seem to execute some control over the distribution of money it seems though only for the benefit of the wealthy. So I suppose you can have some control over situations. What will it take to control hunger, poverty, inequality? We certainly can't seem to control the urge to go shopping except of course through lack of purchasing power but then there is always the credit card.

To be enlightened is to be a social activist in service, not of the self, but in service of poverty stricken humanity. How can one become self enlightened?

In Buddhist philosophy there is no self no soul but only a collective energy manifested through consciousness. In Sulak Sivaraksa's view "both social activism and learning should be based on spiritual development, as awareness that politics, economics, and education are not independent ends in themselves but are interdependent parts of a total human being and human community". A basic human impulse should be to take action on behalf of the poor and oppressed and bring social justice and economic equality within the heartbeat of our solar system. The essence of capitalism is exploitation. The core essence behind all the world's religions is non-exploitation, which is selflessness. For a religion to embrace capitalism is to embrace hypocrisy.

—

Hope I suppose it is simply the act of opening up your heart and loving all in spite of the seeming impossibility of doing such an act in this dimension of space we call the planet earth. Although it does seem hopeless at times for each day I experience earth my heart continues to constrict. It is not easy to truly love and to be honest with yourself.

So we must pull together our creative resources and with our outlandish imaginations create an environment where love can actualize itself by creating a social structure where everyone does not have to be in a constant state of fear as to whether or not they can survive, whether or not they can house and feed their children. I'm not sure what love really is but in this dimension I believe it has something to do with camaraderie, being with friends, sharing resources and dreams. And feeling compassion for suffering people, a compassion that burns with desire to alleviate suffering beyond the demeaning limited handouts of charity and welfare but creating a space of harmonious equality in the acquisition of food, water, housing, and health care.

Equality through sharing the natural resources does not stamp out individuality, we all have distinct personalities and create different things and it's by this that we will be admired and noticed by our peers not by how much more food we eat than the other, not by how big our homes are or how expensive our cars are. To be admired for your house, car, and food only reveals a repressed, un-evolved, cheesy, pedestrian society. We can do better than that. We have the inner freedom to choose our own lives, to find ourselves on the deepest possible level; and only after our partial external masks have been discarded can we recognize our true inner selves enabling us to act spontaneously and authentically in relation to our culture and not be superimposed by a prefabricated definition of the world and of self; this is necessary for the continual unfolding of universal evolution.

We have become machines that acquire machines. The more machines we acquire the more recognition we get from other machines. Boring, uninspired production has turned us into machines. If we bring back imagination we will shed our metal and reveal our souls where pure love dwells patiently awaiting our arrival and return to the space of origination, that of true love which metaphysically is symbolized by the concept of father or mother. Nothing exists in reality but love everything else is just an illusion that became manifested out of fear, fear being the absence of the realization of love. You're a creation of god. You're a being of light, you are the blue light, and you are love. And you don't have to be anything else to be loved. You don't have to do anything special or do anything at all to be loved; you just simply have to be the absolute reality that you are, a pure creation of love in your essential form just like everyone else, no more or no less. True identity only comes from the inner depths of our essence when we splash and play in the living waters.

These personality characteristics of mine are not the type to attract women, especially beautiful women who are attracted to strength and money. So there I remain abandoned from the lustful aura of Eros, without companion to face the internal abyss. To experience suffering is the result of interplay with other states of consciousness. One particular state of conscious existence is only able to exist or be conscious of itself through its interaction with other states of consciousness. Without this interaction with other states of consciousness you would not be self-conscious therefore you would not be participating in a participatory universe. Conscious existence is nothing more than an interactive strategic chess game of conscious emotion seeking pleasure and avoiding suffering. I guess ultimately pleasure seeking comes in packages of social acceptance, needing to be recognized, accepted and loved by others. The rules of this chess game is what gives birth to moral laws and ethics where we dare not step out of line as we may become alienated outcasts with no one to interact with thus causing us to lose our existence with the understanding that consciousness only exists within interaction therefore without interaction we do not exist.

—

People need to stop being materialistic consumer addicts and stop raping the earth. People need to stop being greedy and start sharing in a climate of love and equality. But people want things that make them feel superior. After basic food and shelter everything else is greed. Greed being the number one leading cause of death. It's never good to want anything to bad unless it's is the will of god, and if it's is the will of god it will surely happen. {Jesus said if you have some money, don't lend it out at interest but give to someone who will not return it to you.}

Perhaps things acquired after food & shelter are used to acquire luxury and sex in that order. Sex is a repressed misinterpreted sub-conscious urge so maybe it's to blame for all the world's problems. We need to find new alternative cultural ways to acquire sex other than material success and prostitution. I would sure like a new way to obtain sex because I don't have what it takes to obtain the money to purchase luxury so no sex for me.

I want the world to share equally and live in peace. I don't know why I say that because basically I can't stand people they are all arrogant imbeciles. I don't care about people at all; all I care about is myself. I am as selfish as the next guy. If I want equality it's not because I am a good person it's because I can't stand rich people. I am jealous of rich people because I don't have the confidence or the talent to make the money needed in order to get the nice house, the car and the pretty woman that comes along with it and oh god you know how I adore pretty women. Yes I want sharing and equality not because I am a philanthropist but because of jealousy. I am as greedy as the next guy but just don't have the self-confidence to obtain the goods. Life gave birth to the Greek tragedy. Let alone luxury I am unable at times to even acquire basics. I am miserably poor all alone without a woman. Self-pity adorns me. It must be bad karma I have. I must be a very bad boy.

The system is deeply flawed but it serves its purpose of keeping us distracted from the horrific mystery of existence something to painful to ponder. People don't want free time to contemplate and reflect they don't want to think they just want to be distracted through work and shopping. They don't want freedom because they are afraid of freedom, they don't understand freedom. As Slavoj Zizek uttered, "we feel free because we lack the language to articulate our unfreedom." Genius.

—

I give up. I surrender. I do not know, I do not know that I know I am guilt ridden this I have been schooled since a little boy. The jury has found me guilty for being human. And the penalty given is self-inflicted punishment, eternal damnation in the burning fires of hell for being guilty of sin. Selfishness is the art of being human. I am enveloped in guilt. I am obsessed with it. I breathe it. I lie in it. I thrive off it. It is my whole life it is my name and my god. It is what I worship. It is my prayer. It is how I pray. It is my only hope of redemption and salvation from hell, the eternal inferno, the violence of violence where hate piles up archives of guilty humanity. I am guilt ridden. I eat guilt for breakfast lunch and dinner and I sleep, dream, and make love to it. It incarcerates me. I am not free I am guilty. But even if I were emancipated from it I would choose it. It is mine it is all I own. It is all of me. Oh guilt! Oh guilt who are you friend or foe? I sometimes do not know. Yea I am a selfish mother fucking pig and I feel as guilty as hell for it. And I am afraid I'm going to go to hell if I don't change. I am just a selfish sinful human doomed to eternal hell. Oh god I am trembling in fear with no escape or mercy. I am doomed, scared as hell. I can't breathe. I feel a quiet numbness. Oh death terrifies me. I hate death for death is when I make my final entry into the gates of the 'hell of no return'. Feeling eternal pain, loneliness, terror, fear, alienation, worry, and guilt, suffering eternally forever and ever, my only hope is to believe in god but I can't. I try and try but I can't find faith. I am a screwed man. I am going to hell. Oh god I am so stressed out. I am a wreck. I worry constantly about my inevitable doom. Death is just around the corner coming to see me with its awful stench of terror. God will have no mercy on me for I do no good works of charity. All I do is sin and suffer in my selfishness of sexual pleasure, idolizing my hated ego, the ambivalent paradox of hate and love spilling its red blood of death all over the grave that awaits me or the blazing red & orange incinerator at the devils funeral home. Oh God I am stressed, I do not want to die OK. I repeat I do not want to die. The stress of death is so unbearable that it causes me to fall into the paradox of drinking alcohol. I mean I drink because it helps relieve some of the stress and worry of my inevitable death but the paradox is that by drinking the doctor says I will die sooner. Oh my God it's all hopeless, nothing but suffering every which way I turn. There is no escape from hell, no escape from hell, I have been judged & condemned with a human sentence of eternal damnation in the fires of hell. My ego is my God it is who I worship. It and only it is what I have complete faith in. Oh yes its hopeless I am doomed to endless suffering, no escape, no hope. Oh what a cruel universe that has been created, my doomed soul sentenced to an eternal life of suffering. Oh you cruel universe and your cruel God I wish you would let gravity over rule and contract reverse all the way back to the big bang and let the universe evaporate into nothingness so I won't be created and have to live with this inescapable guilt of being human so as not to have to face eternal damnation.

Oh God I hate churches, I hate the bible it is cruel and mean spirited it is evil. It is in the context of cruel and unusual punishment. It is barbaric, without a doubt a war crime. Oh yes I hate religion and its scriptures in my face every day letting it be known that I am guilty, that my only hope is to turn away from sin and believe in the god almighty. But I can't I try and try but I can't. No matter what I always seem to fall into sin and I try so hard not to. I use will power but nothing works. I always fall into sin. And I always try to believe in God consciously repeating to myself that I believe but it's not real for deep down I have no faith. I want so desperately to believe, I try to believe but nothing works. I mean I sincerely and honestly want to believe for the obvious reason of terminating fear, the fear of hell, eternal damnation, and the fear of not being saved. I am not good enough to be saved. I am only a guilty heathen.

I have been saying I don't believe but perhaps that is a misconception on my part because I must believe in god with complete faith if I believe I'm going to hell because if god is the one who sends you there it therefore must have to exist. I mean if I didn't believe in god I wouldn't believe in hell because the bible says hell is real and you will go there if you don't turn away from sin and pray, believe in Jesus, go to church, etc. So actually if I believe I'm going to hell then I must believe in hell and if I believe in hell I must believe in heaven because you can't have one without the other. The problem with me is that I am convinced beyond any doubt that I am going to hell because I have no confidence to ever believe I would be worthy of heaven, (it's an exclusive club), that I would ever be a contender, a prime candidate to be saved. I can't be saved for I am guilt ridden for hating the bible for the bible reminds me every day that I am doomed to hell forever and ever amen. I face a paradox here meaning that since I hate it I am doomed but if I loved it I wouldn't be doomed but I hate it because of the enormous stress it gives me, stress because of my lack of self confidence. In other words because of my lack of self confidence I know I'm doomed for hell thus causing tremendous anxiety making it difficult for me to love, to love you or me on terms that are hopelessly unobtainable.

Maybe it's perhaps not about going to hell but it's more about getting out of hell because life on earth is hell. It is more unbearable than we ever want to admit to ourselves. We exist in denial going around pretending to ourselves and others that we are happy and life is good, but it is all a lie, life is hell and almost unbearable, that is why so many people numb themselves with vices and sometimes commit suicide. People are just terrified to admit their unhappiness. I drink to escape this unbearable pain of being. No escape or relief at all smack dab in the core of suffering. As I said my main role of suffering is feeling guilt and the fear of death into eternal damnation, I can't bear it. I literally go into the burning chambers of hell. That is why I drink to relieve stress. With alcohol I can sometimes pretend I am momentarily in heaven.

But now I am through with all this, really, for I was able, I'm serious, through the grace of god to witness truth in a recent near death experience where I was engulfed into the bosom of blue light, the essence of God, where it was revealed to me that I will be in heaven as will everyone else no matter how bad or good we are. In other words there is no hell only heaven and everyone is invited. Jesus did not say to believe in god for salvation but meant only for us to believe in order to help relieve the suffering we cause ourselves. So whether you believe in god or not you will go to heaven for there is no other place to go when you die.

It's about going home feeling tired and weary from a long, long journey. If you consider that all things are interconnected as one, as proclaimed by the new science as well as mystical experiences then the concept of hell as in eternal damnation becomes suspect, meaningless. By that I mean if someone is condemned to eternal hell that would mean they would be there eternally, no exceptions. Therefore that would have to mean since we are all connected as one if one person is condemned to eternal hell then we would all have to be, at least a part of us, that doesn't seem probable.

I was hurled like a darting arrow into the center of the universe on my holy conception day when the empiricist measured my sexual bodies, latitude and longitude. In echoing I hear the diverse sounds of despair. Holy Mary mother of God take away the sins of the fall where hatred breeds the toxic waste upon the shores where merchants blaze savoring in their insatiable taste. Politicians squeamish to love sound the horn, the call to war where the soldier awaits in his sheepish state of sleeping beds, where Jesus recruits the poor to enlighten the rich.

—

We take experience and intuition and process it through our cognitive faculties to satisfy the senses and bring fulfillment to the psyche. There is no truth or ultimate meaning but only a drive to gratify the senses and the psyche. It's absurd to think one can know the nature of existence and if one tries he will only come to realize deception and madness. All the world's religions & philosophies are really clueless to the intrinsic nature of reality. Even science ultimately is as well clueless to the underlying workings of the universe. As Einstein mentions "all our science measured against reality is primitive and childlike." The bottom line is nobody really knows what the fuck is going on. It's absolutely amazing to be conscious and alive and not know where you came from or where you are going or as to why you even exist. All beliefs and practices are deceptive cultural taboos rooted in egomania and fear. Perhaps ultimately there is nothing to believe nothing to practice the only thing to do is just breathe. If there is any truth to be realized it is that life is a mystery and all one can do is act from natural intelligence evolving naturally and not under the influence of church and state and its controlling methodologies of Fear, God and Law. So all we can really know is the desire to be happy in body and mind. It's only through the cultivation of individual authenticity can we begin to evolve into higher levels of conscious awareness as a collective species progressing towards happiness.

The problem with society is not a lack of morality but a lack of intelligence as a result of suppressing the natural creative intelligence in the individual. We must, right now, transform together in universal spiritual unity transcending our conditioned patterns of religion, postmodern spirituality, and political ideologies that only alienate and divide rather than encourage the originality of brotherly love. There is no stability in the constant changing now. There is no reality in history, only vague biased memories of a brought on man-made stability of an un-real foundness caused by the eternal freedom of the now that crawls through death unto life fighting a following shadow of a fallen frightened man.

Anarchy let loose as a social phenomenon may serve our desire for pleasure seeking for without rules, regulations, laws, state control and manipulation people can be left alone to be natural and what being natural is would only be for them to decide. I believe in turn that we would then effortlessly gravitate to a more natural state of equilibrium and social cooperation for no other reason than the desire to survive in pleasure. Without natural social interaction and connection the loneliness just eats away at you. Our natural state is individuals cooperating as a whole, not by force or laws but by the natural instinct to survive, survival economics going beyond ideology. It's because of our innate, natural individuality before we were corrupted, in a space closer to origination, that we rebel as youngsters when we are told how to act. I see life I turn away. Oh dear Jesus what a mistake you seemed to have made for forgiveness will only be and always be a game only children play. We build churches and morals as the children laugh & play in our faces every day. The moment of truth is when a child laughs at the parent's mask, the teacher's conditioning, and the preacher's style of speaking. When the child utters or cries out the truth he or she always gets punished.

{His disciples asked him: When will you appear to us? When will you see you? Jesus replied: When you strip naked without shame and trample your clothing underfoot just as little children do, then you will look at the son of the living one without being afraid.}

We as individuals will create a space of cooperation through manifesting many diverse acts of brilliance. People want pleasure, to feel alive and they do this by creating not by following orders and commands of instruction. We are all free to choose and a healthy free individual will always delight in pleasure over repression. Forced cooperation will never work but only come to pass in an open space of pure untainted innocent freedom that will only be birthed through unforced natural anarchy. You can force people to hate but you cannot force them to love.

—

Whatever systemic state of political, economical, theoretical, constitutional consciousness were collectively living in it is not working because I heard the other day from God that every year 11 million children younger than five die needlessly, more than half from hunger related causes. Yes more than 35,000 children under the age of five die every day from preventable causes. Simply parish unnecessarily can you believe that! That is fucked up! The same modern world that gives people tickets for not wearing safety belts because society is so concerned about their safety, that is fucked up, how can such horrific atrocities occur. I certainly can't condone it. But I certainly have done nothing about it. Man I don't want to be that way, that's messed up, being a total asshole. The usual response for such genocidal atrocities is 'that's just the way it is' as professed by the ones who are not hungry. Any economic system that allows for this to occur is messed up. Anybody who says our current economical system is good, that it works, has to be one fucked up son of a bitch asshole. I mean how could anyone promote an economic system that causes 923 million starving people, where every 5 seconds a child dies from hunger. I mean you would have to be one fucked up son of a bitch asshole. I mean could you see it any other way. I mean to allow this to happen is messed up. There can't possibly be any logical rational excuse for its justification other than the fact we are all fucked up assholes. I mean how can you just sit by in your arrogant righteous culture of leisure and comfort and let this shit happen. I mean that is some bad shit you have to be a real asshole to allow this to happen. These people starving to death must hate the fuck out of us for living in comfort, stuffing ourselves to obesity. We don't die from starvation but from over eating, stuffing our fat asses at Denny's eating pancakes smothered in syrup after attending Sunday morning church services. That's fucked up.

We find many reasons to make excuses or to even justify someone going without food and starving either through some scientific philosophical theory, some religious belief or perhaps from some spiritualized new age enlightenment teachings. Although some of these given reasons for the occurrence of poverty and starvation may sound philosophically acceptable that is still no justification to allow for it to continue. We all know deep down in our cognitive hearts there is absolutely no justifiable excuse for starving children. I mean when it comes right down to it in regards to understanding or knowing the mystery of existence nobody really knows what the fuck is going on. But I believe though if we do know one thing it is that there is absolutely no justification for starving children.

So therefore I feel compelled to eradicate suffering from poverty and hunger, whether out of compassion or even selfishness it seems to be the pragmatic thing to do in order to find happiness for myself. Unfortunately the powers that be don't see eye to eye with me on this issue. So I have to knock on the door and become the quintessential salesman and sell my bag of goods to the massive power of the masses. The way I see the situation on my planet is that voluntary poverty is a great virtue but un-voluntary poverty is the great mortal sin of all civilizations. I have nothing against wealth but if it's at the cost of someone else's poverty I will be against it.

To bring about the equal distribution of the natural resources in the context of food, housing and health care to all the peoples of the world does not necessarily have to come from love, philanthropy, or religious pious acts of charity. I believe human intelligence would suffice by simply coming to the logical, rational, pragmatic conclusion that we would all be happier, even the rich, in a social organization constructed to meet every ones needs, leaving no one behind. And I also believe if this ideal ever did come to pass it will be manifested through human intelligence not love for as stupid as we may be we our more capable of acts of intelligence than acts of brotherly love and if and when this happens then and only then will it be possible for us to begin to collectively evolve into higher stages of spiritual love as Teilhard Chardin uttered "science precedes the spiritual." I mean we have to share in order to survive as an interdependent ecological whole. Deep, deep down for the collective expansion of human heart consciousness to manifest every individual that makes up the whole must first have food, shelter, freedom, and leisure time for themselves.

As it is now we basically all work at the same boring job in an intoxicated market economy based on making profit off both essential & nonessential merchandise which creates a cesspool of garbage & trash reeking havoc on the natural eco system, creating nothing of any value but only a cult of anti-aesthetics. 12,000 tons of garbage gets hauled out of New York every day. One third of the people in the world are wading in the garbage while the other one third our sinking head deep into the garbage leaving the remaining one third not even enough garbage to feed on. People need the time to figure out how to crawl out of this garbage. They need the freedom to explore themselves and not be bogged down by some boring, uncreative job that is designed to pay the worker little and the CEO more than he will ever possibly need. We need to find other ways to satisfy the ego's demands other than material accumulation.

—

I feel insecure emotionally out of control like a victim of fate floating through chaos I don't understand anything about life, love or existence; I am always spiritually confused. The harder I try to understand the more confused I become. But that's OK, for I believe if you are not spiritually confused then something must be wrong, perhaps you've become a victim of deception. So I am OK with existing in a constant state of perpetual anxiety and confusion. In this state of consciousness I seem to occasionally simultaneously experience either suffering or pleasure. In my case pleasure is only possible for me when I am wanted by a beautiful, sexy woman. As a matter of fact that is the only experience that gives me pleasure. But unfortunately I don't look or act like the men in the TV shows who own fancy cars, beautifully styled homes, the professional career along with the good looking suit, matching leather brief case, beautiful hair, perfect white teeth, fit body standing 6' tall, just beaming with arrogant confidence. I am none of these things so women avoid and ignore me. I don't seem to have the skill, ability to transform to a level that triggers lust in women. I wish I did. I mean I would sell out in a minute to whatever belief system I cherished within me if it meant I could be with a beautiful woman. Being with a beautiful woman would give me that deep sense of oneness, a divine cosmic interconnectivity, which unconsciously is what we all strive to find. But then there is really no truth behind anything only personalized individual experiences.

We need to find other ways to satisfy the ego's demands other than material accumulation. Ways that are less destructive to the environment and ourselves. Ways that won't harmfully divide people and pit them against one another, meaning of course the side effects of competitive capitalism, competing for the good paying jobs so you can make the monthly payments of success, affording you to live up to the old American adage 'the car gets the girl.' Ultimately this way of life no matter how successful you are does not bring peace and fulfillment to anyone, but only stress, neurosis, and alienation. Its madness, but it's a system that serves the minority elite who have the power and control to maintain and fuel it, if they could only open their eyes and see the light, but I guess the pollution has blocked their view.

—

Corporate, capital finances infiltrated the visionary artist by manufacturing the world of art galleries, high priced paintings, art stars and art connoisseurs. They realized that there would be a small portion of people who would not fit into the status quo because of their artistic genius so they came up with the idea of creating an art world where artist could obtain fame, recognition, and wealth from a pseudo cultural wealthy elite class. What this did was control the fires of creative genius and deter the artist from infiltrating into the status quo with the sole purpose of dismantling it. Thus art as a commodity was born. Fashion-ist-ism. Art then becomes a commodity like generic toothpaste. Avant-garde art is a commodity like non-generic toothpaste, or is the way around, I don't know but does it really matter. Art has come a long ways from the Neolithic days where artist had no concept of art as commodity as in Sony goes graffiti. Our system doesn't foster creativeness but only simulated cunning machines and leaves the creativeness of society to a few handpicked art stars but controlling their creative output by turning art into something to be fashioned, marketed and consumed. Art became contaminated quickly because it is no longer art but only entertainment and entertainment is a fad and fads change in the psyche cross fire of supply and demand. Art though should be timeless just as our divine nature is timeless existing not in the concept of time and place but in the Holy Spirit, holographic packets of energy.

Everything is contaminated. All the things that were once inspiring eventually become contaminated and die, like ending relationships. Inspiration is the Holy Spirit, the essence of life, the fuel for the imagination igniting the poetic genius. To be inspired by a work of art is to embrace the Holy Spirit. To walk in the forest on a rainy Sunday afternoon with your lover now that feels good it can't be classified, it's the essence of just simply being a work of art; being everything and nothing at the same time, existing in pure wisdom without knowing anything.

By partaking in creative endeavors we come to realize we all have different perceptions unable to perceive things the same way so therefore we feel separated from one another but we are only separated by are artistic peculiarities and visions which is manifested in the diverse, dynamic aesthetics of the universe but not so in our underlying reality where it is impossible to explain the classic ineffable mystical experience, the metaphorical tingling sensation upon hearing your favorite song or the feeling you get in your stomach when you have an intense romantic crush on someone. In these fleeting moments we feel connected maybe not specifically to people per se but nonetheless connected to everything. So basically all our outward expressions have no intrinsic substance except of course our omniscient imaginations which, makes me find the statement 'the real world' echoed from the status quo absolutely absurd. It is more along the lines of some quantum mechanical spiritual process dealing with vibrating sub atomic particles and in lieu of its very nature it becomes highly unlikely to be understood or articulated by everyone or anyone even though it's probably a very simple concept, to simple to see. {Jesus said: Recognize what is in front of you, and that which is hidden from you will be revealed to you. Nothing hidden will fail to be displayed.}

I don't know where these thoughts come from because my reality seems a part from what I think. My body stinks, my teeth rot, I need to change because I'm past due, that's why my mind and body are decaying. I've been acting the role of this down and out bohemian, starving artist trip for too long. I need to change maybe go to enlightenment seminars and become some charlatan new age guru, I bet that would get me a beautiful women. I don't know what's wrong I just can't kick this pseudo rebellious counter culture, avant-garde art trip. In the past I would go through my vocations quickly and smoothly right on schedule but I am not changing this time, I'm locked into this trip of being an artist; the eccentric painter, the drunken poet, wanna-be hipster. How frightening if it's my true reality. If so I hope to live to be a happy old painter filled with the innocence of a child, the glowing halo of an eccentric saint as well as portraying the sophistication and genius of Picasso. I don't want to die feeling depressed like the man who worked every day for 50 years and died as soon as he retired because he absolutely did not know what to do with himself.

I have a heart just like yours, and yours, and yours, and everyone else's. It's a heart that is broken into two's, three's, and fours. It's a heart that has been sliced every day since birth. It is a heart that has been shredded and ripped apart at the seams. It is a heart that knows pain, suffering, alienation, loneliness, and it's all it knows. We are a world of broken hearts. The metaphor of life is 'broken heart'. Jesus had a broken heart as he cried passionate pain dying on the cross. His followers suffered broken hearts. The people that murdered him had broken hearts. It was their broken hearts that enabled them to murder him. Jesus was a victim of capital punishment. Broken hearts exist to destroy, one broken heart feeding off another, vampire sucking the hearts blood; the commonality of destruction; cause and effect; the domino effect of broken hearts. The minute we are born our heart is broken in two. Our life mission is then encoded in our DNA, which is to break hearts as we continue to have our own hearts continually break. Break in two to the hundredth power. The star we were born from cracks, splits, crumbles, all dust particles are remnants of broken hearts. Exponentially the heart of the universe breaks as its expansion rapidly increases towards dark, lonely alienation, warm blood turning cold. Our broken hearts are too painful to bear so we live in denial of our broken hearts. We pretend that we are OK by existing in distractions of superficial, sentimental happiness. We can't face our misery so we pretend we are happy by cluttering our life with distraction. It helps feed the denial of how miserably unhappy we are. There are some who see the truth, look beyond the security of denial and see the broken heart and find no alternative but evaporation, especially the very sensitive ones who cannot handle the cosmic violence of broken heartedness.

2

Victims of Crime

We need to share the natural resources equally among ourselves for happiness and worldly fulfillment, maybe even for our survival. In order to do this we are going to have to cut down considerably on our consuming habits especially the products that our considered nonessential commodities. We are going to have to do this so everyone can acquire basic needs. I've heard somewhere that the rich nations would have to cut down their consuming by as much as ninety percent in the next few decades in order to obtain social equity and end environmental destruction. We cannot let one person go without basic needs if we want to survive and find worldly fulfilling happiness. The attitudes surrounding the natural selection process of "survival of the fittest" dog eat dog economics may possibly apply to something, I really don't know. But I certainly do know that the theoretical concept does not apply to humans who are creative, evolving, self-reflective beings conducting order out of disorder through the proper utilization and comprehension of feedback loops. To do otherwise would make us merely instinctual, auto mode self-surviving beasts. We must realize we are more evolved than our behavior leads us to believe as we make our way through the labyrinth of indecency finding clues to our forgotten evolutionary mission that originated before the big bang.

In the future if technology becomes divorced from the military industrial complex maybe then we can create ways to have and enjoy nonessential commodities without experiencing ecocide, and nonessential commodities for everyone leaving no one without. This will make for a happier, healthier, friendlier world to live in. No more need for laws because there will be no more need for war, crime. Without idealism we wouldn't of even made this far. Long Live Idealism. Maybe one day will even become liberated enough to actually enjoy sex.

Twisted minds, to be successful you must work very hard, to be unsuccessful you must work even harder very few people achieve becoming unsuccessful.

People are burned out and stressed out because they either work so fucking hard or they don't work at all. People work hard in the rich nations to acquire more than they need, in the poor nations they work only for food so they don't starve to death. (Over consumption in wealthy nations causes food insecurity in poor nations). People believe they receive acceptance and recognition from peers when they acquire material success. So people acquire material objects not just out of desire for convenience, luxury, and comfort but mostly for recognition and acceptance, this is the core reason for working so hard, which ultimately is for the desire to be loved. This causes a lot of stress because everyone wants love. But if everyone were equally lacking in material accumulation and/or did not need or desire nonessential things then people would not have to acquire them in order to receive peer recognition, acceptance and love. People would be recognized for their own unique individualized personality traits. You wouldn't need to have the financial wealth of Paris Hilton to achieve social fame and recognition you would only need to have the awesome personality of Paris Hilton to elicit such fame.

If we all stopped consuming nonessential commodities we would conserve energy as well as the aesthetic quality of the natural environment that produces the energy. We could find other ways to fulfill our need for pleasure by opening our minds and exercising our imagination. {Jesus said: I will give you that which eyes have not seen, ears have not heard, hands did not touch, and mind have not conceived.}

For those who want the current social, economical, political system to change to an equal, sustainable economy have got to ask themselves the question how much material comfort are you willing to give up and sacrifice for the whole. Am I willing to give up my material comfort both consciously and subconsciously? But for obvious reasons this stuff is going to have to be given up for real change to occur. We have a tendency to blame politicians for the way things are but the only way for things to change is to have the inner willingness to change yourself by making the material sacrifice. Things never change through political revolutions but only through cultural revolutions, which comes about when the status quo breaks down and no longer serves life. I mean you just can't only blame the rich for social inequalities but blame the middle class wanna-be's as well for they are the majority and the majority rules right? Am I right? We do live in a democracy right? So we are going to have to have a cultural revolution in order to create positive evolutionary change. For example in most cases war ultimately insures and maintains our advantageous consumer lifestyle. A poll suggests seventy six percent of the population is opposed to war. But are they really willing to sacrifice deep down, I don't see it, if so you would think you would see a lot more dissent out in the public arena opposing war and material consumption but all I see is complacent apathy and continual shopping. In other words would they be able to give up their consuming lifestyle because that's what war is all about insuring the continuation of their consumer lifestyle, protecting their way of life. A life style that manufactures unemployment, job insecurity, inequality, homelessness, poverty, hunger, competitive division, mental illness, environmental pollution, and all sorts of violence and crime. I believe they would, at least I hope so.

Yes, what we need is a cultural revolution. We really need to get to know and try and understand ourselves at a deeper more intimate level. We need to find out who we really are what we truly want and need. To be more tolerant and excepting of one another, stop telling each other what to do and how to live and begin to start enjoying diversity and listening to one another. Economics has to be more conducive to building healthy, positive, social relations as opposed to competition pitting one against the other for economic gain, dividing instead of unifying. Living more intimately with each other and the environment will naturally transform us to a more just, equal, sustainable economy.

{Jesus spoke: When you understand yourselves you will be understood. And you will realize that you are Sons of the living father. If you do not know yourselves, then you exist in poverty and you are that poverty,}

We need to see through the veils of ignorance and realize once and for all that we our interdependent; our natural state is unity within diversity. Being in a state of unity without diversity causes stagnation, no evolution in other words, we must first blossom with diversity in order to begin to truly evolve in unity as a human species for evolution doesn't even begin to expand, transform until we first meet a minimal level of interconnection manifested within diversity.

For any real lasting, positive transformation to take place in political economics there must be metamorphosis in our collective consciousness, individualized psyche minds intertwining in a holistic communion of multiple dimensions. This transformation will be fueled by the declining desire of the individual in his or hers pursuit for material success and financial wealth, substituting that desire with intimate connection by imagining new forms of celebration in the streets.

The 'powers to be' well not have any control over us when we do not want what they sale us, a psyche boycott of sorts. When we no longer need the American Dream but only crave intimate fulfilling human interaction and pure untainted freedom to creatively express our own true individual uniqueness in unorthodox ways as possible, only then will we truly find peace and happiness and thus begin to expand our human divine collective conscious within the revealing, dynamic, unfolding, creative universe that we are. But again we must first though become emancipated from the limiting bounds of finding ego fulfillment through the accumulation of material objects in the process of sacrificing our lives to the daily drudgery of meaningless work; designed and engineered for the sole purpose of creating capital and only capital. Meaningless job's, sweat shop factories that produce nonessential products that keep the consumption cycle of capitalism going as a necessary means to keep the sweatshop owner wealthy at the expense of the worker and the natural environment. The reward for turning away from materialism will be to not have to spend forty hours or more a week working at boring jobs. In other words you should be able to meet your basic needs while at the same time doing fulfilling creative work, work you freely choose in order to fulfill your personal needs and desires.

—

The quest for the good paying jobs, a perquisite for abundant material accumulation, can be very competitive. Usually a minority percentage will suck it all up leaving the majority with the drudgery of working at meaningless boring jobs with little in return, not enough purchasing power for material luxury but only enough for less than minimal survival, lacking behind in health care, nutritious calories and living in depressing substandard housing. The current economic system needs to be turned upside down and shaking or just simply deleted and replaced with a system that meets every ones basic needs. {Jesus said: I have thrown fire on the world. Look! I watch it until it blazes.}

Capitalism is reeking havoc on the world and undermining the democratic process. It's a death culture; anybody who becomes a card-carrying member dies in mind, body, and soul. We must begin to deal with the side effects sooner than later if the human species is going to survive. The only way to deal with this pandemic is not through political revolution but only through a cultural revolution can such a deeply rooted problem be eradicated. What a cultural revolution involves is a radical shift in the human psyche, a mental attitude that turns away from consumer culture and material wealth.

It is difficult for consumption serves a need for distraction; it frees the mind from obsessing over ones problems, which is the recipe for addiction. So in order to stop consumption you have to find other ways for people to become distracted from their problems (ironically though it is probably consumer culture that causes all their problems) and hopefully replace consumerism with a healthy distraction. Possibly an effective substitute would probably be community celebration, creating the space for multiple diverse interaction, communicating ideas, exploring new ways for individual/collective fulfillment and pleasure, sharing visionary uniqueness, creating community excitement with unlimited diverse activities and varying interests.

To kick-start this cultural evolution a new generation of mainstream pop/counter culture marketers must market the aesthetics of 'less is more' and no longer be hoodwinked by the commoditization of dissent. We need to create a media pop-culture where the younger generation says it's not kool to experience material abundance that time would be better spent igniting the spark of imagination by pursuing unlimited possibilities such as experimentation with altered states of consciousness by participating ayahuasca rituals. In solitude you go into yourself in order to get out of yourself into one love. You find that all and nothing encounter one another and are one and the same. The less material possessions one has the kooler one is, this allows for more individualization and less cloning, the commercial axiom will change from 'just do it' to 'less is more.' It's about being able to feel absolute connection with others while at the same time not having to conform, but only be yourself.

—

It seems that the overwhelming majority of people don't seem to care about the state of the world or take any personal initiative to modify their living habits in order to create a healthier, aesthetic environment. Is it because the current social economic infrastructure has had such a negative effect on the psychic consciousness of people that they have basically lost all respect for life including their own? I mean would people now ever collectively comply again with a 55 MPH speed limit to conserve energy as they did back in the seventies a time perhaps when people had a deeper since of human value in their relation to ecosystems? I mean as it is now they don't even drive the posted speed limit but exceed way past it with gas guzzling SUV'S and they rarely get speeding tickets for the police exceed the speed limit as well. Life now has become meaningless and valueless. I mean how can one conclude otherwise when you consider the negative damages that have occurred to our ecosystem as a result of our consuming habits. It has also made its imprint on our soul manifested through the negative side effects of stress, anxiety, depression, divorce, suicide, poor health, not to even mention the horrific spiritual crisis of the statistical fact that 923 million people live in devastating poverty and hunger indirectly as a result of our global economical over consuming market culture.

Most Americans generally want peace and harmony in the world but their basically not willing to sacrifice anything for it. Maybe deep down people do want to change but they can't because they've become more or less dependent on the current economic infrastructure in order to survive. So maybe it's not that they don't care they just don't have the opportunity for change. They feel they have no way out or alternative but to work at jobs they don't like. They have to own a car and drive fast in order to get to work on time. And with what little money they may have left after they pay their basic survival bills they spend it on products, products that give them social, cultural identity, the spectacle of belonging to Costco.

—

When it comes to the equal distribution of the natural resources it's really not a complicated task to achieve in regards to pragmatic, political, economic theory. The only real thing that stands in the way making it difficult to implement is a lack of will. Once you have the will the infrastructure of such a provocative economic plan will easily fall into place with only basic social economic engineering. But without a collective, deep genuine desire it will never work. So all that is needed is the will not some ingenious, grandiose economic theory coming out of the halls of academia. The will must come first then everything else will fall into place. The will can come from many diverse motivations, such as a religious/spiritual epiphany that advocates sharing, compassion, love, brotherhood, altruism or it may come from a more humanitarian, pragmatic, scientific perspective derived through analytical, intellectual discourse rationalizing that this will be the most effective way to conduct economics in order to actualize optimum social contentment and/or perhaps more importantly it may come from the motivation for our desire to survive as a human species. Or it could simply come from a more selfish individualized perspective where each individual (including the rich) comes to realize that they will actually be happier under a system of sharing, believing his/hers personal selfish needs will actually be more easily obtained in a ecological community without crime, pollution, stress, violence, competition, and terrorism etc. so on and so on. One thing for sure it would make it easier for me to get a girlfriend because most girls in our economic culture prefer men with money in order to help them fulfill their desires of social identity embellished in material accumulation.

Spirituality it is not about aspiring to become good it's

about expanding conscious awareness and as a result some goodness may manifest out of this process, the goodness coming from the awareness of our interdependence. When an individual realizes that it's not about him/her but about the whole he/she has made a major breakthrough on his/her journey to the realization that he/she is love. Individuals need to work together in creating a better whole. For one without the other is no one at all.

—

I am a little man who has a saddened bitter heart saddened and bitter by my unfulfilled desires. The desire to unite with a sexy, sensual, beautiful women in lustful romance, stroking the flesh into the inner ecstasy of divine origin, digging deep through the cells and membranes to the inner core of existence, being unto being flesh unto flesh. Yes the treasure lies deep from within from without from that which is all. Is this what I seek the wrong path through eternity? A path that is self-indulging catering to the flesh of the ego, or could it be a righteous path leading to divine ecstasy. I don't' know for I have not found a beautiful woman who freely chooses to love me to prove the hypothesis right or wrong. So how shall I act? Do I act in a way that comes natural to me or do I act in a way that I believe will attract the attention of a woman I deeply desire so that she will desire me for who I am not. Obviously the latter because I lack the self -confidence that she would love me for who I am.

Technicalities bore me I am a romanticist, a dreamer, a free thinker, not a doer. Yea I just like to think but it makes me feel guilty, shameful, because it doesn't have a by-product of material substance. It is not looked upon as an act of doing from the perspective of a Christian, puritanical work ethic, unless of course your paid money for doing it. It is laziness idleness of the devil. But free thinking is by no means effortless it takes a lot of energy especially when you try to form and structuralize. Yes I am a free thinker who drinks antidotaly to the pain of life. My life is financial poverty and emotional chaos. My virtue and religion is striving for liberated authenticity.

People are supposed to be thinkers. To be a philosopher is the most natural state of being for humans. We are not doers we are thinkers. We are not designed to live in an instinctual auto mode like animals because we have been gifted a sense of self-reflection, a cosmic awareness, in other words we are natural mystics, star travelers. But our economic structure lures, mesmerizes us into a hypnotic mode of doers not thinkers but only a means of production for the accumulation of capital wealth. We are not production and service workers we are creative thinkers. We need to rethink our roles in society and the greater cosmos and come to a deeper understanding of what are purpose is as human beings in this space of consciousness we exist in. We need to create an economic system that gives us more time for free thinking and less time spent for physical survival and productive output. People need healthy food, shelter, and aesthetic environment to wonder and ponder their nature. The basics needed for earthly longevity. We need to organize an economic system that enables every individual access to basic needs as well as free time to be free and create. It just seems so strange to me the way humans live. Why did they choose this way to function as a society? What is the point of living if you spend all your time trying to distract yourself from thinking about the awesome mystery of life in all its vastness?

Guns, swords, knives and spoons, spoons to scoop in order to eat, to eat the kill, dripping red liquid fumes burning industrial waste. Tortured hope the sacrifice of original sin. March on, march on you happy soldier, happy, loyal, obedient soldier through the debris of limbs, brains, splattered guts, decapitated heads, and broken eyes, broken homes, broken children, broken mothers, fathers, cousins, uncles, grandparents, broken buildings, statues, trophies, churches, schools, broken televisions, broken cars, broken hospitals, court houses, prisons, grave yards, broken banks, super markets, broken condominiums, gardens, libraries, refugee camps and dogs. Don't look back soldier keep marching on ahead for there is money to be made and many things to buy, screaming lined silver. Don't look back soldier stay filed in line on the path to glory.

There are a lot of human beings out there living in devastating poverty. The reason it exists and continues to exist is because the human beings who are not living in poverty don't care their unconcerned, distracted and detached about the hardships of the poor only working towards their own financial success and interest in the application of spiritual cosmetics. I would say out of all the people in the world who are not living in poverty only about less than one percent really care about the poor and try to actually do something to end their hardships. And to those who show concern by giving a few crumbs of charity once in a while to ease their Christian guilt don't really count as caring, besides charity actually exacerbates the problem instead of addressing it with real solutions that would finally end inequality and poverty once and for all.

In good times when you hear from the media how good and prosperous the economy is doing, how people are doing better than ever and unemployment is low, well if you just happen to be someone that is not doing so well where you can't pay your bills, you can't pay your rent, you're sick but can't afford to go to the doctor even though you have a job that you work hard at everyday; a job that causes stress, a job you just don't like, you are going to feel depressed. Or maybe you are someone who doesn't even have a job and has given up looking, so when you hear on the television everyday that the economy is great it's going to make you feel even more depressed, like a big loser. And because you feel so much shame about yourself your probably aren't going to go out and express yourself, broadcast your situation to the world especially to your peers because you believe your situation must be your fault not the systems and this is exactly how the system wants you to feel and think.

Alienation is the nature of meaningless work. Sweatshop factories produce nonessential products with cheap labor, creating wealth at the top and poverty at the bottom. The movement of capital causes job insecurity in the developed countries and deplorable working conditions in the developing countries. Work sucks; we need work with more meaning and depth beyond our demeaning material culture, work that manifests a society of decency, dignity, morality, harmony, peace, equality, aesthetics, enlightenment, and human inspiration in the arts, science and culture for everyone. Work that excites the imagination to the mere wonderment of the nature of the universe and our true roles we play in it. But know we only offer a methodology of drudgery, work that turns people into ignorant, emotionless cyborgs.

The nature of work has to be radically changed. We need to develop technology where we don't have to spend so much time working in order to survive but able to spend more time developing our minds, our spiritual insights, our artistic creative instincts, fully transcending and expanding our cosmic awareness to higher levels of experiencing joy and happiness. Just as we automated the manufacturing industry we need to automate the service industry so nobody in the world has to work anymore at unfulfilling boring jobs but instead be able to use their free time to creatively grow and expand their inner selves, cultivating understanding between one another, growing in peace and harmony. Where an individual would have a lot more time to pursue their own interests whether it be the arts, entertainment, science, hiking, gardening, sex, sports, traveling, whatever they choose the possibilities are unlimited. And what necessary jobs that do remain that require our labor that might be considered unpleasant will have to be shared by everyone.

—

Maybe I am wrong in my perception that everyone is really unhappy and only pretending to be happy. Maybe there are people unlike me who really are genuinely happy. Maybe finding happiness in their selective micro world but perhaps only because of the narrow parameters of that world they reside in; but perhaps if their narrow micro world of happiness would collapse and if they were expelled from their gated community becoming exposed to different stimuli they might freak out.

There is a person who claims to be happy and upon observing this guy he does indeed seem to appear happy. He is very successful and has a very good job in which he is financially rewarded and recognized, praised by his peers for his success. He has a lot of confidence in himself. He also has a beautiful wife whom he proudly displays as if a trophy. He owns a beautifully designed large home in a gated community. He owns a beautiful new car that transports him around his beautifully landscaped neighborhood. He is basically enclosed in his micro world of happiness and beauty. His only exposure to the macro world is through television and movies even though he does exercise some control over what he sees through the limited free choice of selective viewing. The other possible exposure to the macro world is when he has to leave his neighborhood and drive on the freeway or international travel where he may encounter unusual disgusting entities emanating from the macro world. What does this man feel when he occasionally witnesses suffering in his fellow humans, pity, compassion, empathy, injustice or does he feel superiority and even anger or disgust towards such entities as an unpleasant nuisance? He pretty much has the freedom, power and wealth to create his own sublime micro world in an aesthetically pleasing environment. This man is genuinely happy and the only thing that could possibly make him unhappy would to be to lose all that he has and be discarded into the macro world with all its elements of despair, displeasure and suffering aesthetics. So you would have to imagine that he must feel some discomfort and anxiety maybe outright fear at the thought of losing it all, to be cast out into the macro world unprotected from his private micro world. You would think that this anxiety must disrupt his pleasurable life of feeling complete fulfilling happiness maybe even bringing enough insecurity to the point of absolute suppressed madness. There would have to be an end to all the suffering encountered in the macro world for him to have any possibility of finding complete happiness. Because of our interdependent web of collective consciousness if someone is suffering you will suffer as well indirectly or subconsciously.

When you have desires for material abundance, recognition from peers, fame and so forth and when you acquire these things then you are going to feel good about yourself as being successful and you will perceive people to think about you in a positive way as well. On the other hand if you don't acquire material abundance and success you are going to have a low opinion of yourself feeling like a failure therefore making it difficult for you to interact with other people because you think they see you as you see yourself, a loser. But either outcome is ultimately the same because they are both about the egocentric material self, they are not about the true divine self that you are. So what one must do to really be fulfilled and truly free is to substitute the egocentric self, whether negative or positive, for the true divine self which is not self concerned but unknowingly detached from the world existing in pure freedom. A state of being that gives of itself in the form of pure divine love. The mind is not the real self but only an instrument to realize and awaken the divine self so as to be in that space where you won't be concerned about how much you're loved but only about how much you love, nor concerned about how often people think about you but only about how much you think and care for others. You will only see the goodness in others and never pass judgment on anyone. {Jesus said: I stood in the midst of the world. I came to them in the flesh. I found all of them drunk. I found not one of them to be thirsty. My soul was saddened by the sons of men for they are mentally blind. They do not see that they have come into the world empty and they will go out of the world empty. But they are drunk. When they sober up they will repent.}

If there is a true desire to find peace there must be a desire to find us within ourselves. We must create our own spiritual path and not be hoodwinked by a prescribed religion of spiritual matriculation. There must be a single personal spiritual vision for everyone, an esoteric vision of the whole created by the individual. This is needed in order to find true peace and harmony among each other for you can't use someone else's spiritual beliefs. When groups of people come together and practice the same dogmatisms in many cases it ultimately propagates fundamentalism, social retardation, intolerance, division and violence. A look back through time reveals this. When every individual develops their own spiritual vision or truth, only then, through tolerance, will we come together in unity. People think religions form fellowship and unity, they may within their congregation find superficial unity but this quasi unity eventually only breeds intolerance towards others, causing separation between the people of the world, which leads inevitably, indirectly, subconsciously to violence and war.

People need to discover their innate spiritual insight within themselves, a vision giving them guidance on their personal journey to an intrinsic spiritual freedom of nonidentity. This authenticity will allow for true spiritual evolution. If someone upon hearing the details of a personal spiritual vision through someone sharing their revelation, and they say, "that sounds helpful to me I think I will follow their vision," if so they will only be deceiving themselves blindly going down the wrong spiritual path delaying his or hers evolution to origination. You cannot borrow someone else's vision for yourself, it is a spiritual trap to attach on and follow someone else's vision. That is common sense. This is what the original teachings of Jesus said, not to follow him but do as he says and follow your true spiritual self within yourself and you will find the truth as he has. (Remember everything is a paradox.) Jesus is implying to us that he is not here to tell us how to follow rules but to encourage us to find the truth by breaking the rules, which lies hidden and dormant within us until we discover it. You must find your own god and your own belief. By all means find your own inner spiritual path a personal path that can only be revealed to you. Only when everyone comes to realize his or her personal god, spiritual vision, can we find world peace. The world will only realize interconnectedness and peace when there is not one God but six billion different Gods, or six billion different visions of the one God. So the greatness of the master prophets is in their spiritual awareness and insight of informing us not to follow them but to follow our true inner visions where the truth awaits for everyone. So what we have to do is create a socially organized environment where people have the freedom, the time, the resources to find themselves, exercising their individual creativeness to seek their personal spiritual essence. And everyone must have tolerance in allowing every individual to express and practice their personal spirituality no matter how peculiar, odd, or unorthodox it may appear as long as their practice does not impinge upon anyone else's freedom to act. You could say true freedom is not freedom of religion but freedom from religion.

—

I had found a woman who seemed to like me romantically. I really liked her and got caught up in the romantic fantasy of it all and therefore really splurged and spent all the money I had saved up with a little help from a credit card. It was a wonderful time of fine dining, lots of wine, great sex, even attended the symphony and ballet. It all felt like a dream until reality set in. When the money ran out she dumped me. She basically indirectly informed me that she only wanted to see me if I was able to continue to take her out and do things that cost money, but I ran out of money, end of story. She was though genuinely disappointed because I believe she really did enjoy my company. So instead of completely dumping me she offered me encouragement and direction to change my financial impotency. She pleaded with me to change by changing my lifestyle, to stay focused and build up my confidence, set my standards and goals higher, become empowered and work hard, suggesting all the most popular self help books, the ones that guarantee to turn empower you on the path to financial success, think positive, stay focused, affirm, visualize, financial abundance will come to you. Our culture propagates this psyche phenomenon fueled by the propaganda media networks singing the lyrics of equal opportunity and liberty. Positive thinking and hard work will guarantee everyone the American dream. I tried but after two days I could not take it anymore so I told her to take that lifestyle she was demanding of me and go away that I would rather stay home and masturbate. She said she was merely suggesting that I should try harder to get a good paying job.

I just hate all that crap about self empowerment, self-confidence and positive attitude, especially when it comes at you disguised as a spiritual package selling financial abundance through spiritual enlightenment via spiritual marketing. All it's really about is consumer culture. Whatever turns you on but it bores the shit out of me.

In my search for women I inadvertently got involved with some spiritual practice where the believers would chant for hours seeking empowerment and wealth, it was a mix of Tony Robbins and multi-level marketing. Even though I am powerless unlike most of you I don't want or need power. Yes I would like to transform the world up a notch or two, increase the vibration laying the foundation for environmental sustainability and social equality. But that won't be accomplished through power because power is the problem. No matter how it is manifested it is the very essence of the problem. It can only be accomplished through passive, creative, sensitive interaction. The world will never be saved or changed though the cultivation of power. Self-empowered confident competitive people always have to get into an argument, which sometimes turns into violence. The core root of world wars is empowerment. {Jesus said: Whoever has become rich should rule. Whoever has power should renounce it.}

3

Chances are

There is no reason to have any government or social organization other than for the pragmatic methodological need to equally serve everyone his or her fair share of the planets natural resources. When it comes to the natural resources no one should have more than the other for creation and evolution could not have possibly attended for it to be that way. The natural resources are a divine gift to be shared. But this spiritual concept of a social construction can never be forced upon any one it can only come to be realized from within ones consciousness eventually permeating to the collective will. It will never come to pass through violent revolution if it is to be authentic.

There are well over 6 billion people in a world with a limited amount of natural resources for everyone to survive on so to get a better understanding of the social complexity involved let's scale down the world from a macro to a micro perspective. Let's say there are 3 people on a very small island that only has enough resources for minimal survival. Do you think they would fight for the resources, survival of the fittest free market style, or would they equally share? Let's see if they competed for the limited resources the strongest and the most cunning would get more than he/or she needed and all that would be left would only be enough for one more to survive. The stronger of the remaining two takes what's left of the remaining resources, which isn't much, leaving nothing for the weakest one therefore parishes. Because of the unsustainable over indulging habits practiced by the strongest one all the resources eventually disappear leaving nothing for no one therefore the remaining two eventually parish as well. This is a story of competition, a social organization of conquer and divide, strife, distrust, separation and division, a life without purpose or meaning but only isolation and loneliness, a recipe for war, violence and death.

If things were different and they had a social blueprint of cooperation, equally sharing and sustaining the limited resources I believe they would all be better off. They would have harmony and companionship instead of social strife, separation and death. They would form community giving a sense of meaning and purpose to their lives beyond material survival. They would not only be able to share the resources but also share ideas enabling growth and development to blossom both individually as well as collectively, allowing for continual survival and evolutionary expansion. Whether it's 6 billion people living on the whole planet or 3 people on an island it's simply the same thing, harmony or strife, survival or extinction. {Therefore I say that if one is unified one will be filled with light, but if one is divided one will be filled with darkness}. Jesus spoke}

The bottom line is if we are going to survive we are going to have to equally share. We must equally distribute the natural resources among every single living creature and the only way we can do this is by every individuals willing desire. This most certainly can never be achieved through totalitarian force. It will come through an expansion of awareness in the desire to be free and happy and the realization that this will be the only way to survive with happiness. We will eventually come to realize that we have been living in the illusive nature of free market capitalism, controlled and manipulated by the power of social acceptance, military technology, mass media, entertainment, commercialism, and wanna-be soccer moms. Comfort defined as success and conformity. Success and conformity is the foundation of the illusion. Conformity propagates violence; conformity is slavery, programmable software.

This is no utopia but just a different way of conducting economics, no big deal. I am not talking about utopia but creating an environment of free expression where people aren't burdened by the time consuming unnecessary acts of social and physical survival. Where people have time to contemplate and process the existential tragedies of life we all face and have no control over such as a loss of loved ones, terminal illness, loss of our body functions and broken hearts, family & community relationships, sexual relationships and spiritual exploration etc. etc. It's just about creating a better space to deal with the existential crisis of encountering the mysterious nature of life such as contemplating the unconscionable tinniest of our planet when scaled against the vastness of the whole universe. There is much to ponder and wonder about, the awe of it all. Every second is a miracle but do we realize it when we spend so many hours of our life producing and buying nonessential commodities as if we believed we really do not have any other choice. We spend our whole life in the service of others producing their wealth with our labor leaving no time for ourselves, only to be rewarded with a life of drudgery and insecurity. This, what we have been born into is not true reality but only a culturally conditioned perception of reality. Our reality is defined by our culture, that is why when shown a film on hygiene, the primitive tribal people when afterwards were asked what they had seen, they responded by saying they saw a chicken. Why only a chicken, because the material in the film was not a part of their particular, perceptual, cultural reality?

—

True freedom is diversity within unity, not conformity. Diversity needs to flourish from individual to individual, from community to community. So if there be one, diversity should be the number one social norm. Yes we can all agree that life is a mystery so therefore we should have the time and freedom to seek and find uncovering the mystery of personal truth and fulfillment. {Jesus said: The seeker should not stop until he finds. When he does find, he will be disturbed. After having been disturbed, he will be astonished. Then he will reign over everything.} From day one society tells us how to think, feel and act even our deepest insights are manipulated from religion telling us how to find truth, enlightenment, and God. This possibly might not work so we have to discover truth for ourselves. As mentioned, religious and spiritual teachings only act as an anomaly and divert us from our personal vision of truth and awareness. This must and only can be our personal responsibility to find truth for ourselves and this can only be done in a state of pure freedom beyond the constraints of society. Freedom is constricted by rejection.

So when I advocate sharing the natural resources and living sustainable I am not advocating conformity to a particular lifestyle, as you might imagine it to be nothing more than a commune of long haired unshaven hippies living a nonmaterial lifestyle of organic farming, playing drums, and dancing naked. But quite the contrary my idea could not be further from the truth. That is just one of many particular lifestyles, you don't have to act and dress like a hippie to live in a world that practices equality, sharing and sustainable living. People can live any way they want they only have to share and sustain. If they want to hang out at the bowling alley, drink beer and smoke cigarettes that's OK they can do whatever they want. The bottom line is we share and sustain in order to survive, to avoid ultimate environmental destruction and/or nuclear war. We do this out of the simple desire of wanting to live instead of die. Anybody can live as they please any life style they want the only thing they have to conform too is the natural law of cooperation, a law of nature one must live by in order for the whole to survive.

We will design a system that gives everybody their fair share of the natural resources within the mathematical laws of sustainable living. And do this through means of advanced technology so everyone has only to put in a minimal amount of time and energy to produce the needed resources for survival leaving plenty of free time to pursue their own personal lifestyles, interest and hobbies. We don't all have to act the same and we should not because we advocate diversity and tolerance as everyone sets out on their own path following their own dream. It's all about unity within diversity. You could make the argument that such a life of individual diversity could naturally lead to mystical oneness.

Freedom and diversity is a good thing because it encourages creative evolution, not stagnation but an evolving, unfolding human consciousness. Growing in conscious awareness can bring us amazing wonderful discoveries in science and human relationships, things never before imagined, helping the ecosystem to evolve ever more. This is why we need more time to cultivate our non-physical minds and imaginations, set free from long hours of demeaning work and the hypnotic lure of material commercialization. It's not work that is bad it's the type of work that we have been doing. Working is fun, creative and healthy, as creative beings we were designed to work. We just need to work less and have more time for recreation and relaxation. I am sure through new advances in technology no one would have to work more than 2 hours a day, probably even less as technology continues to advance; doing the necessary work of processing the earth's resources in an environmentally safe sustainable way so every man, woman and child in the whole wide world will have enough to meet their basic needs for healthy survival.

Yes I believe if this ever truly came to pass we would continually advance in technology, and I don't mean military technology but holistic, life-affirming technology because living in a world of equality we wouldn't need any more weapons. I'm talking about healthy technology, a technology that is in harmony with the ecosystem, technology that serves all life and not just for the benefits of an elitist minority. Equality and justice leads to environmental aesthetics.

Another reason we would advance so much is everyone would be using and expanding their creative imaginations through playful work. By this I mean they say most people only use a small portion of their brain so as we begin to develop our consciousness through the study of non-physical matter our creative intelligence will blossom. But there is even more, for example under the current system there is an enormous waste of creative genius, only a very limited number of people are giving the opportunity to develop their minds from early education on to halls of higher education. Just think if everyone had that same opportunity how many more geniuses, Einstein's, would be discovered. In a social structure of equality everyone would have the opportunity to exercise and manifest his or her intellect. This would have absolutely amazing results in the evolutionary advancement of humanity. I mean as I speak right now there are many, many, minds brilliant minds being wasted away all over the world, spanning the globe from the ghettos of America to the villages of South East Asia. In developing countries close to 72 million children are not enrolled in school, and there are 781 million illiterate adults worldwide. What a waste, paving the way for more war, poverty and the disease of hunger. What an astonishing atrocity, a tragic mistake, a theory gone wrong, competition over cooperation. The way the system works now is to insure that everybody doesn't have a PhD because of everybody had a PhD then a PhD would no longer come to mean anything in other words making it irrelevant as a means to market yourself ahead of the next guy in order to gain financial success in the professional career of free market competition.

The world has voted and has chosen freedom and competition over cooperation and sacrifice. But when you think about it is it really freedom they have chosen when you consider the world is constantly enslaved to a military budget in an ever increasing insecure world spending multitudes more on military defense than developmental assistance, health and education. Is it freedom when many people are forced either through extreme poverty or national mandatory laws to pick up a gun and go to war and kill someone they don't even know. Is that freedom where thousands of children currently serve in the military, more than 50-armed groups in 15 countries? Is it freedom when 923 million people across the world are hungry and every day 16 thousand children under the age of 5 die from hunger-related causes? Is it freedom when your only means of survival is a credit card with high interest rates? Is that freedom when you are constantly bombarded from a manipulative, controlling, misinformation media telling you how to live and conform? Is it freedom being overworked at meaningless jobs to pay for non-essential crap you have been lead to believe you need in order to be accepted and loved? Is it freedom when so many people can't find work at all and are forced to a life of devastating poverty, or maybe working, even long hours, but only receiving poverty wages, barely enough to sustain themselves or their family? Is it freedom when the landlord has forbidden me to smoke in my apartment or not allow any family to come from a far and stay over a few nights with me? Is it freedom when I can't even rent an apartment because I don't have good credit, (health care debt) or a high enough income to write down on the rental application to qualify for a substandard rundown apartment complex? I mean I have never been late on rent in my in whole life but giving your word doesn't matter to the property owner. We are not a free society because nothing is free meaning how can anything be free if the ethos of our society is a "price tag?"

Freedom is an indefinable concept absolutely void of any real meaning at best a subtle manifestation of relative perception. Individual consideration is collective freedom. When political economic theory comes up with the buddy system, I'll give you your space if you give me mine, I'll scratch your back if you scratch mine so on and so on we may then begin to collectively seek the lowest common denominator of all possible restraints to freedom, James's pragmatism if you will. The buddy system works by trying to create a humane concept of freedom that has the least possible amount of restraints on the individual, creating a space with minimal distractions to clear the mind, to expand the mind deep within and come out with pure self expression.

So you have to have some restraints on the individual in order for every individual to reach the highest possible sum of free expression. For example let's take the automobile, which has always been the icon of American individualism, an unbounded free spirit, sounds good but there is problem

94

with this picture and that would be automobile exhaust. Carbon dioxide emissions infringes upon everybody's individual freedom and rights because they have no choice but to inhale the exhaust which hinders their need and desire for healthy air, everyone has to breathe the air. Air pollution worldwide is estimated to cause 3 million deaths a year, in the US alone air pollution causes 70,000 deaths a year compared to 45,000 deaths from auto related accidents, and it even goes further than that when you take in the consequential effects carbon emissions is having on global climate change. So the symbol of freedom inadvertently turns out to be enormous restraint on everyone in the whole world in the suppression of clean air, not free to breathe clean air. Now on the other hand smoking tobacco is OK for the individual to do because tobacco doesn't hurt anyone but the smoker. Oh I know there are a lot of people that would disagree but come on if second hand smoke was a danger to our health then we would have all been dead a long time ago from car exhaust. The point being this type of freedom ends up being no freedom. So if in your freedom you do an act that hinders someone else's freedom then you have canceled out the others freedom. So freedom rests on a fine line it's all about balance, the yin & yang of freedom. Too much freedom for one takes away freedom from the other.

Freedom as it is now always comes down to money, the more money you have the more freedom you have, the freedom to buy property so nobody can tell you that you can't smoke in your home or have guests over or have a dog. And even if you have the money to purchase freedom you inadvertently become a systemic slave to the unavoidable duties and requirements necessary to make the money to buy the freedom. Without balance there can be no freedom. Freedom is really more about cooperation than competition. Competition causes imbalance cooperation causes balance so therefore cooperation causes freedom. The only freedom in the world as it is now is the freedom to become wealthy but very few have the freedom to acquire wealth. So in this world freedom becomes synonymous with money, which ends up not being freedom at all but only competition, which cancels out freedom. Plus if someone has more money than they need that means someone else has less money than they need therefore taken away that person opportunity for freedom and in some cases even taking away someone's basic needs such as adequate health care, nutritious food, education and housing, ultimately taking away their freedom to survive.

In this world we all desire wealth and power and spend all are time competing for it, we have been conditioned to believe this is what we need and want and the more we have the happier we are. We have been taught from an early age to compete for the same prize. Is this truly what the majority wants and freely chooses? I doubt the existential, innate, authenticity of such a choice and believe we have all been hoodwinked into thinking its free choice. If there honestly is free choice how could it be possible everybody would want to choose the same thing, have the same goals. In a truly free society there would be a lot more diversity as to what each individual chooses. I believe the American mind has been manipulated, conditioned and controlled to all want the same thing this is not freedom this is not free choice. Freedom can't coincide with a society that is constantly manipulated by a massive propaganda campaign continually flowing out of the mainstream media, funded by addictive consumers engaging in their desire to acquire. The establishment preaches liberty from the political pulpit while behind closed doors it cunningly and deceitfully acts to suppress the people by producing social milieus of deception. This of course is not true for every individual there are those who think outside the mall so there is hope that someday we will acquire true freedom, as mentioned above, can only come out of cooperation. Even if you do succeed in acquiring large sums of wealth are you then honestly free when you have to live in arm guarded gated communities limiting the amount of space you can comfortably walk around out of fear of being mugged by the have-not's, the side effects of competitive injustice.

And there is little freedom in finding and choosing the kind of work you want to do with the limited job opportunities available, especially without quality training or education. This is not true freedom but only a limited field of choice. You should not have to compete for any job; you should be able to do whatever you want, what is best suited for you. Everybody should have the freedom not only to work but also to work at doing what he or she loves.

Freedom does though have to come with sacrifice and that sacrifice is cooperation. We are all going to have to sacrifice a little if we are ever going to experience an optimum level of freedom, which balances on a very fine line, that space of freedom where we encounter the least amount of possible anomalies to intrinsic self expression.

—

This manipulation of the American mind is all fear based, insinuating that there isn't enough to go around for everyone so you must work hard and compete or you will become destitute. And this fear of scarcity breeds greed, fear has always been an effective way to control people because where there is fear there is no freedom, freedom and fear cannot coexist. But there are enough natural resources for everyone to meet their basic needs but unfortunately under the current social, economic, unsustainable infrastructure there is not enough because of all the enormous waste, the imbalance of power and distribution, incompetent greedy exploitation along with the absolute barbarism of "profit before people" trickledown economics.

The system is based on people working and earning money to buy products. The products are made cheaply as possible in order to be sold at prices affordable to the buyer but still allowing for large profits for the product producer. By making the product as cheaply as possible it opens the market to people with limited income. And most of these products are not even needed for survival but only nonessential crap like exercising machines that only get used for a few months then put away in the garage with all the other crap. I am not saying we don't need any nonessential commodities we just have to be much more selective with our limited resources and present technology at least at this particular moment in evolution.

I would no doubt be content and satisfied with the current social structure if I had a good job, a nice home in a safe area that was beautifully landscaped, had excellent health care, always had a nice new car and free of stress to maintain this life of comfort. But I don't have this and I am a sore loser so I want it to change. And whether or not I like the current economic trend it really doesn't matter. By that I mean if we want to survive as a species were going to have to change our economic customs and traditions because the population is expanding in a world of shrinking resources. As the resources become less available people will compete more intensely for them, from communities to nations to continents, all over the world, and this competition will only lead to violence, war and possibly nuclear annihilation. And our survival is not only threatened over competition for finite resources but also through the unsustainable misuse and mismanagement of these resources causing irreparable environmental damage. Whether it's from inequity or misuse of the natural resources or both it will all come down to ecocide. We made some bad choices and may have blown it. So we are going to have no choice but to change if we all want to survive. I just hope the world has enough freedom to make that choice. We can survive we just need the will and the freedom to choose.

—

The world is ugly, recognizable by poverty, violence and pollution, overwhelmed with a sense of despair and hopelessness for any lasting positive change. In order for the world to increase its aesthetic values it must open its heart and embrace equality in the form of cooperation opposed to competition. For individualized competition in the struggle for economic survival is creating a landscape of despair. We must awaken our senses and expand our perceptions so we may enter into the sublimity of community consciousness. We must clean house turning it inside out and upside down shaking out all the debris of despair. The whole anti-aesthetic cultural psyche must transform its perceptions of success as it is now so narrowly defined, limited to material luxury as the social norm of pop culture, pleasure and entertainment.

In order to create an aesthetic landscape we must first bring an end to inequality the main cause of poverty, violence, and environmental pollution, (Let's face it the root cause of pollution is competition.) And to do this we must radically change our economic social infrastructure and begin equally sharing the earth's natural resources. In other words as mentioned the rich nations will need to cut down their consumption of the earths' resources by ninety percent in order to fairly and equally share with the rest of the world without causing environmental destruction. America alone is only five percent of the population but uses twenty five to forty percent of world's resources. This must be done if we are to meet every individual's basic needs for survival. But this will not be easy for our whole cultural psyche has been deeply conditioned to believe the individuals quest for fulfillment and pleasure can only be realized through over abundant material accumulation. Can we Change? It will not be easy. Striving for success is deeply embedded in all of us and some will go to great lengths to achieve it by any means necessary. Without this accomplishment we feel empty, incomplete, left behind, nothing but a loser. We believe that this is just a fact of life that there can be no other way, it's the law of the jungle, survival of the fittest, compete and win or go away and die, this has become our self realization of absolute reality, the zeitgeist of our times. {But Jesus tells us: the Kingdom of the Father is like a woman who is carrying a jar full of grain. As she walked along a handle of her jar broke off and grain trickled out, but she didn't notice. When she arrived in her house, she put the jar down and found it empty.}

From a western perspective this is what is known as our 'way of life' what the patriotic propaganda media machine claims to be the reason why the Middle Eastern Muslims hate us so much and want to destroy us. It does appear though that western civilization and its way of life may be destroying its self only to be avoided by a radical directional change in political will. Our way of life is a highly innocuous level of carbon emissions and it's having a negative effect on the whole world through its presence in the earth's atmosphere. Basically the production and use of oil with its negative environmental side effects is the process that is fueling our way of life and we have always had to put our claws down hard and scratch the face of the Middle Eastern landscape in order to maintain this way of life via access to sizable pools of oil. The irony here is that we have to control and exploit the Middle East to maintain our way of life, the way of life that the Middle East sees as a threat to their way of life. Also when you consider that the technology is there for alternative forms of energy other than oil but still insist on continuing to use oil you would have to conclude that the objective is to use every last drop of oil until it is all gone and not until then and only then will we begin to use other forms of energy. Even though the oil is causing global warming and tension throughout the world in the competitive conquest over its limited supply, which could possibly lead to nuclear war were still not turning away from it. And why is this? Because of money and all the power, wealth, luxury, and false security that comes from oil. So when asked the question by an alien observer what defines our way of life it can only honestly answer greed. Greed is at the core of our way of life and it is very close to destroying the whole planet.

Taken in this context how can you expect there not to be enormous anger at our way of life by the people of the Middle East when we go into their back yards and homes, put our noses in their business and exploit them for our own gain with our enormous power and wealth. Do you see them over here in our backyards trying to exploit our way of life sucking up all our resources for their own selfish financial gain? It doesn't take a highly developed cognitive process to figure this out any simple mind could come to this logical conclusion: the powerful underhandedly exploit the world's natural resources and the peoples that inhabit the land in order to sustain their insatiable greed.

The world is really not that complicated all we have to do is immediately cut down our carbon emission ninety percent in and begin using alternative forms of renewable energy that our much less toxic to the natural environment. And make peace with the Middle East through reparation, reconciliation and by getting out of their faces and leaving them alone to live their culture however they so choose.

It has been stated by the scientific community that global warming could have devastating effects on the planet and its inhabitants. Years and years of pollutant waste since the industrial revolution have been spewing carbon emissions into the atmosphere, and with the increasing population along with their machines the pollution has now reached levels increasingly threatening to our ability to survive. Some alarmists conclude that it may be too late to do anything about it. The media is finally giving it some attention and people are now beginning to talk. Most of the talk is about blaming the politicians and leaders for not doing anything about it or at least not enough. Observing away from all the hype and buzz what we have is a basic problem with a simple solution, "just stop polluting" it's just that simple. If we have to wait for our politicians to get the OK from the corporate money suppliers to take action against global warming we will not survive. But we don't need to depend on the politicians to initiate legislative policy to curb global pollution all we have to do is just collectively stop driving, using fossil fuels and cutting down forests, it's that simple.

In all fairness though they can't help what they do because they are sick with addiction, no different than any other kind of addiction. There particular addiction is power and wealth, known as greed. So it can only be up to the people to change the direction of global pollution. So why are we not acting, what is stopping us from wanting to survive and for the possibility of our grandchildren to survive? The obvious reason being of course as everyone says, it's the 'economy.' The economy would crash if everyone stopped polluting and consuming, we would lose our jobs and even if we had a job we wouldn't be able to get there without our beloved cars for transport. But it's the unsustainable economy that's threatening us. The hypothesis is without cars, consuming, and working at environmental destructive jobs we would not be able to survive, such an irony seeing that our choice to not change our way of life will inevitably destroy the whole planet making a difficult for anyone to own anything or even perhaps survive, including the corporate elites. This is the neurosis of free market capitalism. Everyone is addicted one way or another to material consumption and wealth and for those who do not have wealth the fantasy to achieve it lures them in. We are basically in denial of global pollution, we hear about it but we really don't listen, we should be able to see it but we can't because we have turned off our conscious. So it's a simple proposition; if we want to survive we just simply stop polluting. It won't be easy, we will have to undergo a radical shift in lifestyle and bear an enormous sacrifice but if we do we will survive. It's that simple. But in the long run we will all be better off and much happier. And if the debate remains as to whether global warming is harmful or not it doesn't really matter anyway because our toxic industrialization is going to harm us and the planet one way or another through its continuation of unsustainable capital growth.

I went swimming in the ocean in southern cal and the water was so stinking dirty there was literally garbage floating around giving me this awful toxic taste in my mouth. The dirty polluted ocean contrasted with the surrounding beach town which was real nice, clean, and quaint. The homes were charming with their Spanish red tiled roofs, the area was beautifully landscaped, lots of colorful flowers, a very affluent community, the people had nice cars and wore nice clothes everything was nice except for the polluted ocean water. I could not understand how they could put up with that dirty Water. The irony is it is there affluent lifestyle that is indirectly causing the polluted water. It's kind of like the child pushing everything under the bed when the parent orders them to clean their bedroom.

—

We as a human species are not only lacking in benevolence and unity we our also lacking in intelligence. We simply are not intelligent enough to figure out that the possibility for happiness and fulfillment might be better served if we completely transformed our geo-political social structure to a more humane space of equality and cooperation. Why do people want competition in work it just causes stress and stress kills, I can see competition in sports for fun but competition in survival that is barbaric. Work should never be looked upon as a necessary evil one must do in order to survive. We don't have to work in order to survive we need to play in order to survive. Work is a joy, a beautiful, fruitful creative act that gives us great fulfillment. We are confused if we are only motivated to work under the condition that we will be given money or material rewards, work can only be an effortless act of joy, always playful, not as a means to an end. Believe me when people begin to work only for the joy of creation all their physical and mental needs will be given to them indirectly from our creator. God's work was playful, creating for joy, so should our work be. There should be no separation between work and play. We are just going to have to wake up and see the light or our planet will rant in its frustration at our ignorance in the form of increasing natural disasters.

We need to reinvent new forms of understanding and communication, a new language that enables us to express to one another how we really feel, that we don't want to live in fear, that all we really want is to be loved and excepted by who we really are and not the roles the status quo has assigned us. How will we be able to convince an individual or family with a rewarding successful high paying job, very popular with many admiring peers, big expensive home, expensive cars and lots of nonessential commodities to give it all up in exchange for a nonmaterial, non-consuming life style with equal distribution, living in modest eco housing and the only means of transportation being either mass transit or a bicycle? You tell them they will be happier. Or ask them if they want to survive or not, for their lifestyle of an unbalanced concentration of wealth will eventually lead to their demise. *I think they will just laugh and say "you're funny".*

———

I am an artist, a painter, working in the realms of the sublime trying to create aesthetic, cultural landscapes. My medium is social activism. As an artist I am constantly being criticized by the cultural elite and the middle class wanna-be's for my efforts to construct an economical system that will create an aesthetic environment. I just desire an aesthetic world and I feel if we simply stopped consuming and polluting and shared the natural resources equally the world would rise in aesthetic value. The rich don't want to lose their riches and the middle and upper classes don't want to lose their comfort and the lower classes don't want to miss out on the slight possibility at a chance of moving up the ladder, fulfilling their dreams and desires of obtaining wealth either through hard work, crime, or winning the lottery.

We have over 6 billion people on a planet with finite resources. As it stands now in order for everyone to have their fair share of God's gifts the people living in developed countries, as I emphasis again, would have to possibly cut down their consumption by ninety percent. I don't think this will happen anytime soon if indeed ever. That would be a sound bet. So that means if they don't cut back their habitual consumption in lieu of dwindling resources the people that have little to nothing will probably parish. I guess what I am saying it all comes down to the ratio: the amount that everybody is willing to give up as to the number of people perishing. I think the people who have a lot now will be willing to give up a little and conserve but not for the benefit of all but only to insure a continual adequate supply for themselves and their peers leaving nothing for the rest. Their motivation for conservation is not holistic but based on separation thinking only of their own long term needs.

Being green is becoming popular for consumers as they conserve and recycle using more energy efficient products from light bulbs to automobiles. And their efforts thus far are really nothing more than novelty not having any real substantial effect because their still in a state of denial in their over consuming habits. But all these efforts at being green are useless if they are not intended holistically. Because the planet will only survive as a holistic process anything less we will all eventually parish. A construction company advertised its business as building green homes. They showed pictures of some of the single-family homes they built, they may have been energy efficient but they were too big. Two families could have easily live in that large of space. Building a big green house for a single family is not quite so green after all when you factor in the overconsumption of building materials. The construction company advertises itself as green but it is really not so green after all but only green enough to conserve enough energy for a portion of the whole. But we have to conserve holistically by obviously designing living spaces that are our smaller if we are to survive as a whole species.

We all desire good paying fulltime jobs so we can buy more products than we need; and usually how much we get paid takes priority over what we do. We suffer at our jobs so we can enjoy our time off spending the money we make, ultimately leading to a life devoid of authentic social relations, purpose or meaning but only a life of parking, shopping and spending. Let's face it we are not happy but overworked, overweight, under paid, depressed and stressed out. The competition is fierce and the battle grows more and more intense every day, the ones who find material success only later become disillusioned overtaking by a deep empty feeling, a life without soul value.

The battle for success is very competitive in a world of limited products. It's a harsh, cruel, insensitive world we have created for ourselves driven no less by pride, greed, and Power. We have not been educated through wisdom but only trained as consuming desensitized robots programmed for production & promotion absent a heart without feeling or character.

To know when you have enough is to be rich
Lao tzu

4

Rich in soul poor in gold

We have just come into the new millennium and the general forecast on the horizon is looking bleak. The world is feeling tension with seemingly never ending violence as competitive war rages on in its competitive pursuit of exhausted resources and dwindling oil reserves, the most powerful usually winning the grand prize. Genocide is becoming a common word as we humans continue to become more and more desensitized and spiritually numb. The Military industrial complex marches on to war making large sums of money, the only thing keeping the economy afloat. Many people living in exploitation and devastating poverty cannot take it anymore and are beginning to speak out and fight back with sticks and stones for their inalienable rights. Astronomical debt both public and private, off the charts trade deficits, excessive military spending and tax breaks for rich along with corporate casino gambling is causing an ideological, economical breakdown, unseen turmoil lures just around the corner, watch out middle class. There are winners and there are losers, everyone fears becoming a loser and there are always more losers than winners. Many of the losers don't even end up with enough money to feed themselves probably therefore parish. It must be so sad to see your child die from starvation. The world order though is starting to feel the squeeze with its workers becoming discontent from many years of stagnant wages along with rising prices in housing, food and energy, especially the rapidly rising cost of gas.

The world is changing fast and not for the better. Free market globalization is the rule of the day. A policy manufactured by and for the world's elites the powerful and the strong, a corpotocracy gone mad with greed. This is having an enormous effect on the whole planet causing great wealth at the top and devastating poverty at the bottom, the gap between the rich and the poor is growing wider every day. The people at the bottom of the economic scale can hardly afford to eat with the rising cost of food. International free trade is causing pollution along with climate change and the mass migration of third world people leaving their homeland searching for livelihood in the rich countries only place they could find a less than minimal living wage. These people suffer many hardships being far away from their families and have to deal with anger, racism, and hatred from the rich countries working class, a competitive global society of nation against nation, community against community, race against race, family against family, woman against man, individual against individual.

The world is just becoming a chaotic mess of insecurity over taking by greed and power, CEO's laughing madly all the way to the bank, leaving nothing for the rest, nothing but insecurity and a few dollars a day to buy nothing but nonessential junk at corporate mega-stores sprawled out across the global landscape. The environment is becoming a chemically saturated toxic wasteland from misuse and over use of the natural resources. Global warming is causing severe storms, the sea water is rising while the fresh water on the land is evaporating and desserts are increasing in size as the forests continue to be cut down. Our food and water is increasingly becoming unsafe to eat and drink, an increasing number of biological species are becoming extinct. Growth and production remains the legislation of the day, "We need to Grow the Economy, Bring me the Money, Work Harder, Work Harder, We must meet our Quotas" "Work, work, work, Spend, spend, spend. Buy, buy, and Buy." The GNP sets the standards for social quality. The company's motto to the shareholders "profit before people" marches on in glory.

It's scary out there, poverty, homelessness and the prison industrial complex keeps growing while education and health care keeps shrinking. People are stressed out and scared, alienated, feeling lonely in a world lacking in the proper humane use of modern technology. Hate crimes and racial tension are on the rise. The people who cannot find that desired plateau of material success become despaired and hopeless. The world is controlled through fear; people are becoming less and less inclined to speak out as civil liberties are being stripped away. Throughout the world families and communities are coming apart along with nation states, as has elsewhere been noted indicating the first warning signs of a failing civilization. It's all a game in a battling gladiator arena the better trained the better ability to win, produce and acquire. We only teach our children to adapt to the system not to develop the necessary critical aptitude to transform the system. One should not memorize a Zen Koan but only listen to it.

Enough is enough we have got to tear it all down and recreate an infrastructure that is in harmony with a sustainable living planet that allows for everyone on the planet their fair share of the earth's resources. And only by doing this will we break free from the cyclical treadmill and begin a new journey in creative evolution. Such a paradigm shift will expand our consciousness giving us new forms of technology never before imagined, creating abundance for everyone not just the select few. This shift in consciousness will give us the wisdom and knowledge to effectively share the natural resources equally among the world's population of plants, animals and humans finally giving us a way out of violence, competitive war, and environmental destruction. {They asked him: when is the Kingdom coming? He replied: It is not coming in an easily observable manner.

114

People will not be saying, "Look, it's over here" or Look, it's over there. "Rather, the Kingdom of the father is already spread out on the earth, and people aren't aware of it.}

So the plan is to split up the resources equally with over 6 billion people and do it with the least minimal effect on individual liberties and freedom. I suppose not an easy task to accomplish but I believe we can do it if we have the will to survive and want to be free. Yes we must share the resources but it would be the up most importance to do it in a way that allows for the highest possible amount of individual freedom. I have always cherished individual freedom, hoots to Patrick Henry "give me liberty or give me death". I have always hated and feared authority, especially institutionalized authority. I would find it a total nightmare to be living under a totalitarian government. So there is a fine line between sharing equally and individual freedom. But sharing the earth's resources should not have to invade your liberties. I mean it seems common social sense that everybody should have their fair share, to be allocated in a sustainable, efficient, self organizing manner, not static but always changing and evolving through the feedback of multiple creative efforts. Basically people would have the freedom, especially in a world that is ever more learning the aesthetic quality of acceptance and diversity, to do whatever they want although with limited material goods. This would be a never-ending process of continually creating systems that would allow for the highest possible amount of individual freedom and fulfillment. It's about creating the best possible environment for freedom to thrive, freedom from slave labor and drudgery.

It won't be organized around a static manifesto of strict rules and regulations but an inspiring pulse of forever changing systems always creating the best possible results from a decentralized self-organizing multiplicity. Basically you would not have the liberty to take away somebody else's fair share giving you more than you need and leaving someone else with less than they need throwing the whole eco system out of balance. And it would be necessary for everyone to put in their fair share of work to produce the needed resources, a system designed on efficiency and fairness, placing individual talent in the proper place allowing for optimum human fulfillment. Why do people want competition and suffering over cooperation and pleasure? Why do we believe it can be no other way?

The amount of time working would be greatly reduced curing us of many work related health problems. There would be full employment, everybody working part time sharing the work giving us a lot more free time for ourselves. Yes the concept of work would radically change for the labor involved in extracting the earth's resources would be evenly shared as well as the rewards of that labor. Continual technological advancements in robotic design would also give us increasingly more free time from labor allowing even more time to pursue personal interest and hobbies or just lie in a field and dream staring up at the clouds floating in the clear blue sky or gazing out at the night stars in all their awe and wonder. Money would no longer be necessary for individual motivation; the desire for individual material abundance would be replaced by holistic abundance. Work would always be done in a playful fun way. Yes people would have a lot of time for themselves to pursue their own interest whatever it may be.

It would be difficult to distribute the work fairly but it could be eventually worked out to an optimum degree of individual satisfaction. Although everybody does their fair share of work there will always be those who want complete freedom and not have to answer to anyone, it's OK that's just the way some people are going to be. But they will not have to work at all because with everybody working, full employment; there will be more workers than needed. So if someone doesn't want to work they will not have to. But I guarantee most people will want to work, they don't want too much freedom because they don't know how to deal with it, but they will learn. And as artificial intelligence continued to advance robots would be able to do more and more of the less desired laborious tasks. Everybody would find their perfect niche to help out according to their skills, but more importantly to their desires, with dignity and purpose. Everybody would have a sense of purpose from old to the young, from the strong to the weak. No more unemployment or welfare, despair, worry, stress, alienation and homelessness, but only participation, for no one will be left behind. Remember a chain is only as strong as its weakest link so therefore we would become a healthy multi-cultural human species. There will be many jobs to do but they will all be for the purpose of creating an optimum quality of life that is earth friendly, sustainable, and individually fulfilling, an economy for the people, the land, the air, the water, the animals and the trees that's not based on profit, an earth economy that will nourish the soul through right livelihood, a labor of love and celebration. Yes in such a scenario people would want to work more than was necessary just for the pleasure of working. The pleasure of working hard in the hot sun not worrying about having enough money to pay the bills at the end of the month but only thinking about how wonderful that cold beer is going to taste at the end of the day sitting in the warm summer shade with good friends, talking, laughing, enjoying the camaraderie. Work will not be an unfortunate necessity as we think of it now. Freedom from longs hours of drudgery will give us time for self-reflection, contemplating the awe and wonder of existence. Creating different perceptions of reality other than parental induction; learning how to create magic through the expansion of consciousness and the stimulation of the cerebral cortex; creating unprecedented, exhilarating forms of entertainment.

People would also not need to work as much as before because we will no longer be an economy of 'desire to acquire' in other words working overtime to make more money to buy more stuff. Making a lot of unnecessary products requires a lot of unnecessary hours of labor to produce them. Capital is created on waste through making more products than needed. For products now are not designed to last a long time or be recycled because when a product breaks and isn't recycled there needs to be another product produced to replace it and this creates more sales therefore more profit for the product producer. It's an economy built on waste.

You really can't write a manifesto for such an ideal as sharing the natural resources but more importantly what you do need is the will, the will to share the resource, and allowing for a free flowing self organizing system to create that will. Many problems would obviously arise but they could all be worked out in time with local cooperation. One obvious problem would be limited products due to sustainability; the planet just doesn't have enough for everyone to own a musical instrument. But obviously music is important for an evolving, creative culture so if there were not enough musical instruments for everyone who desired one then they would have to be shared in a systemic way that allowed for the highest possible output of individual pleasure and creativity. It's really very simple it all comes down to what you learned in preschool, that it's 'nice to share', that it is 'better to share', 'good to share', that it is 'civil to share', we just have to take this concept to heart where it becomes a natural act and not just a sentimental meaningless social platitude only to be exercised by preschool children.

Pleasure boats are another material desire that could easily be shared by everyone. I mean you go to any marina on any given day and you will notice that over ninety percent of the boats in the marina are not being used; they just sit there floating. Is it possible that it is more about the prestige that comes with owning a boat or luxury yacht than the actual desire to repeatedly take it out for a sail? So many times I would go down to the marina and just look at all the boats just sitting there being wasted wishing how I could use one of those boats to go sailing. It would be nice if they were there for the people to share, especially the people who really genuinely loved sailing but could never afford to buy a boat. So we should share the use of the boats, it would kind of be like renting a boat instead of owning one except the difference being in this paradigm of economic transfiguration there would be no rental fee.

Since we are at the marina let's talk about the beach, everybody wants to live by the beach especially in warmer climates. This is a potential problem because of limited shoreline. One thing that would allow for more beach area and access would be to not have any structures within two miles of the beach. This would leave plenty of space for camping creating a more natural environment.

The beach town as well would be a highly desirable place to live, but as with the shoreline there wouldn't be enough space to accommodate everyone. You would have to devise a way to fairly allocate this living space. Perhaps one way to decide who gets to live closest to the beach is by the amount of time a person would spend at the beach, for example surfers would have a priority because they would probably use the beach a lot more than others. So the more you use the beach the closer you get to live by it. And if it turns out extraordinary amount of people equally use the beach then you would have to design an infrastructure for living that would be able to accommodate a large amount of people and one obvious way is to build smaller living spaces among many other possibilities. It's never going to be a perfect world, utopias are illusive, but what are you going to do. We are just trying to create a space so we can all survive with the highest possible amount of dignity and pleasure, all these problems can be worked out and not just by one person but many people involved in the process of creating community infrastructure. The important thing is to have a multiplicity of creative minds coming out of self-organizing systems. This would not be a hierarchical process of a few people at the top in positions of power coming up with the ideas and making the final decisions but a fully participatory process with all minds functioning in cohesion. When you have fully participatory systems no minds are wasted allowing space for brilliant creative ideas of genius to flourish and multiply, ideas never before imagined. So when problems arise, no matter what their context, they will eventually be solved through the participatory process, the multiplicity of creative minds. The old clique "two heads are better than one" will now be

6 billion heads are better than 1 million.

It all comes down to cooperation being the key element to survival and healthy longevity. But I believe competition can't be completely eliminated and I don't think it should, I just don't think competition will work when it comes to global survival. But aside from that healthy competition can serve a purpose. Competition can be lot of fun in games and sports, there's nothing wrong about competing for fun. And competition can be very growth oriented in dealing with the problems that arise out of one's ego. Because competition usually means win or lose and this can have an enormous effect on the ego both negative and positive, this can ignite psychological and spiritual growth in healthy ways. Competition is hard to be avoided anyway by the mere fact we are sexual beings, there is an incredible amount of competition in the mating process, along with jealousy, and through this process spiritual, psychological growth will spawn within the entanglement of ego and unity. So competition is full of life being both painful and joyous but when it comes to global survival and limited resources cooperation is the only way.

Everybody can live anywhere they want in the world no one competing for space and for the places that attracted a large portion of people the logistical problems would just have to be worked out as already mentioned. Can you imagine how wonderful it would be to live anywhere your heart desires? Cross cultural integration would work will in a global society of full participation. How wonderful of an experience to have cross-cultural interaction all over the world, sharing culture, customs, food, entertainment, art, sports, as well as ancient wisdom. But ethnic roots would always be encouraged and preserved for a continuation of cultural diversity. This would be awesome; wisdom would flourish everywhere continually creating paradigm shifts through the exchange of ideas, visions, and feelings. I can see all the happy, smiling children running around laughing and playing, growing and sharing. School would be fun compared to now, which are now nothing more than military training schools training militants to compete in a monetary global economy.

People would not only be able to live anywhere they wanted but also be able to travel anywhere they wanted. Cultural acceptance would prevail and racism would dissolve because people would be equal. When a person travels to different parts of the world they would be fully accepted and welcomed without fear of resentment, crime or violence. They would be able to fully intermix with the people, their land and customs with joy and inspiration.

The particular locations that attracted a lot of people would basically become urban cultural centers. Existing cities would basically have to be torn down and rebuilt using architectural building designs that accommodated large numbers of people in limited space. Creating sheltered spaces synthesized with natural plantation and vegetable gardens. Fruit trees would be planted all over the city with no wasted fruit as you see so much of now in people's backyards, creating an environment that allowed for highest possible degree of health, harmony and aesthetics. Architecture designed for social interaction but also for the necessity of individual privacy and quiet solitude. For existing cities being completely redesigned and rebuilt all the buildings would be torn down and recycled except for the buildings with ancient sacred value as well as the buildings displaying historical aesthetics.

Theses urban complexes would be cultural centers of art, entertainment, concert halls, theaters, sporting events, nightclubs, cafes, libraries, museums and universities. The cities would be designed to be ecological sustainable catering to diversity and the quality of human life instead of commerce and finance, without shopping centers pedaling nonessential commodities ultimately producing only toxic waste. There would be no more wasted space such as abandoned, vacate buildings or miles and miles of six lane boulevards with accompanying parking lots. Transportation would only be by mass transit, bicycles or walking.

Just outside the urban centers would be many individual small farming communities, crops that would produce most of the food for the populated urban centers, done of course using organic ecological sustainable growing systems. The small villages would be known for their celebrative festivals of music, dance, great food and lots of homemade beer and wine.

There would also be a lot of smaller towns and villages spread throughout the whole world, less populated areas for those who preferred a more natural quiet environment than the more populated urban areas could allow for. The living structures in these smaller communities could be larger than the ones in the urban centers because of the availability of more space but still very modest in size for global sustainability. The smaller villages would have a lot more individual expression in architecture and those who wanted could design and build their own home. For those people who wanted to live a more hermetic lifestyle could build homes in very secluded mountain areas or out in the desert unconfined from anything other than practicing ecological sustainable living within their natural environment.

These community designs are just possible suggestions that would probably never happen as described but the important thing is to know is where there is will there is a way. Possibly urban centers would shrink in population as people became more spread out in smaller rural settings for they would no longer be forced to live in urban areas out of the need to find employment as it is now. The bottom line is that for any positive change there must be collective sacrifice, sacrificing material comfort for community harmony throughout the world, finally coming to realize that only when everybody becomes poor there will be no more poor.

—

With such a radical shift in our social structure of

putting people before profit peace before war and fusing together scientific research with spiritual wisdom we will begin to make absolutely amazing discoveries. The entire scientific community would be working in cooperation instead of destructive competition creating anything from unlimited clean energy to metaphysical self-healing techniques. Would you rather have a doctor operate on you who is motivated by money or one who is motivated by the love of being a doctor? The new discoveries in technology will give us all we need to live fruitful, healthy lives. But the important main ingredient for this to happen is global equality for all, an honest sharing of the natural resources becoming truly embedded in everyday reality. Such a paradigm shift supersedes socialism, capitalism, totalitarianism, democracy, as we know of them now. This will never come to pass through violent revolution, even though history reveals that that violent revolution has usually been the most utilized way for change to occur, but none the less, history also reveals that such revolutions are usually short lived: meaning the oppressed inevitably become the suppressers.

So what might we need for such a radical change to come to pass? This will only happen when the powers to be, the elitist oligarchy, federal reserve bank, the filthy rich, the upper, middle, and lower class wanna-be's all have a change of heart, an absolute shift/and or expansion in collective consciousness, nothing less short of a miracle, divine intervention if you will, and come to realize such a change in social structure, beyond any doubt, will simply give them more happiness and fulfillment than the current social structure affords them. So ironically the selfish desire for individual happiness and fulfillment will only come to be realized, obtained through the unselfish act of sharing. We have the imagination/soul to transform our present state of existence, our perceptions of reality. We have the resources and ability to end hunger, disease, poverty, homelessness and war all we lack now is the will to make it happen. We also lack the belief that it can happen but there are no absolute truths behind belief systems they are only culturally constructed so anything and everything is possible and believable.

—

Many preachers are sounding the alarm to their flock of sheep from the Christian pulpit that the end times our near, be prepared for the day of rapture. Broadcasting that we must turn away from sin and turn to Jesus and that only by believing in Jesus as the one and only savior can we be saved from the fires of hell and lifted up to the kingdom of heaven. I find this interpretation to be suspect. It seems to me what Jesus meant, what he was actually saying, is that by believing in what he taught you will become enlightened, relieving one from the enormous stress and suffering one experiences in lower states of earth consciousness. It's not about believing in him but believing in his teachings, believing in what he brings to our conscious awareness.

And what did he reveal to us? {His disciples asked him: When will the dead rest? When will the new world arrive? He replied: That which you are waiting for has come, but you don't see it.}

5

waiting for eons

Yes it has been revealed the universe is a dynamic, evolving organism not static but fully alive continually creating out of a vacuum of energy impatiently awaiting our awakening. Creation and evolution are synonymous. Are we now ready to evolve into the consciousness of collective love or are we to remain forever in separation consciousness, which shows its ugly face in the political mechanics of 'conquer and divide.' The US as a beacon of democracy and equality, protector of human rights, has the opportunity to push the human ideal of global peace and equality throughout the world. However, will the US live up to its spiritual calling? Or will it follow the path of history becoming another victim of power and greed thus self – destruct just as the empires preceding it have?

It's been almost a century since the Copenhagen Interpretation of quantum mechanics, these initial discoveries; which showed the limitations of human, logical, rational thought; are just beginning to have an effect on contemporary culture where once again we see a reawakening of the right side of our brain. It is most crucial amidst the crisis of these times to develop the essence of our etheric nature, which is to process and maximize the mystical, intuitive and emotional. This will help us realize the epistemological insights of the wisdom to be found in the irrational, non-linear and chaotic as credible forms of understanding.

New discoveries in astrophysics are stirring up our hearts and waking up our curious minds. I believe the paranormal; the irrational imagination will no longer be 'social taboo' but rather embraced as a key element in scientific inquiry and social transformation. Our cold rigid mechanical bodies will melt down along with our dogmatic religions paving the way for a collective mystical experience taking us beyond the bounds of hierarchical patriarchy and a Cartesian rationalization of love into the pure experience of love. The day of harvest is upon us the fruit of wisdom is ripe so let's all begin to feast on the gift of light and drink from the living waters.

Perhaps it might help the process if our public and private institutions were to catch up with postmodern science. It seems they are still living in the fading shadows of a static, mechanical, dualistic, Cartesian perception of reality. This social, philosophical, mythological construct of controlling, manipulating and exploiting the natural planet as well as the social landscape for ill gain seems to serve the institutions of plutocracy, who feed off spiritually numbed consumers, but in no way shape or form does it appear to serve the soul of our planet and the majority of its inhabitants. Our religious institutions have fallen as well as Walter Brueggeman brings to our awareness: "The contemporary American church is so largely enculturated to the American ethos of consumerism that it has little power to believe or act....enculturation is true not only of the institution of the church but of us as persons. Our consciousness has been claimed by false perceptions idolatrous systems of language and rhetoric."

Four centuries into the 'age of enlightenment' and all we have to show for it is a culture of machinery and weapons. In the process we have become machines ourselves, cold, calculated, analytical robots being served our daily doses of Prozac. We have lost touch with our inner mystical imaginations. We have lost all sense of meaning for machines have no values. The machine creates nonessential products in which the advertiser sells to addicted consumers who in turn become machines. As machines we find our identity in the products we consume and we relate to one another through this super imposed identity.

The age of enlightenment has brought us to the edge of spiritual bankruptcy, (maximum share holder profit) putting profit before earth and its inhabitants. In its efforts to control and manipulate a mechanical predictable Newtonian universe corporate society and the institutions of public space have discounted the inherent value to be found in the paranormal, in feelings, emotions and psyche intuition as a credible cognition and placed false trust in analytical dissection, calculated forms of numbers, charts, and graphs. Classical physics turned the universe into a preprogrammed automated vending machine, separating the parts to find out what makes it tick, inadvertently separating people from each other, the universe and God. This is especially true today in relation to community; we have replaced sensual, physical community, (community of the flesh), with a cyber community rendering us even more isolated and alienated from one another as well as the natural earth. This is concerning for I believe it is in the space of sensual community that our humanist values are deepened.

Newtonian physics, still embedded in our institutions, is claiming to be based on 'absolute truth', that there is a separate objective independent reality that we can observe objectively. This is problematic in that it stunts evolutionary growth by giving credibility to the status quo (real world) and its institutions. The status quo is stifled from transforming because its perception of absolute reality is still based on classical physics even though classical physics has become to be seen as a very limited perception of so called reality. It appears that our public institutions are falling behind contemporary science. Is this perhaps because a change in the perception of reality would not benefit the institutions of commerce and the politics of greed and power?

It is in our imagination where the fires of creativity burn.

Without the romantic passion of the imagination we will not evolve but only remain conditionally oppressed. The dualism created by assuming an objective reality of separated parts can only suppress the imagination and propagate disunity.

The negative side effects of Cartesian philosophy have taken a toll on our lands, oceans, skies, and wildlife. We as a human race have littered our space with garbage, the garbage of over-abundance for a few at the cost of poverty for the rest, the garbage of separation, division and alienation as revealed in ourselves, our families and our communities. If we are going to survive as a human species we are going to have to change our institutions today from competition to cooperation for it may be too late if we wait until tomorrow.

The story of the universe is the story of creation, a continual process of annihilation and rebirthing. Virtual subatomic particles seemingly appear out of nothingness only to immediately disappear. As a species we are a collective conscious form of energy always striving to be as we trip, fall down and pull ourselves right back up again just as a child learns to walk. We somehow seem to create order out of disorder to only come upon more disorder. Seemingly, we intuitively know that within our mysterious depths we simultaneously have control and no control over our lives, paradox lies in the center of mystery. It is through this mystery that we develop our faith and trust in an unfolding universe pulsating with love, surrendering with open arms to this chaotic, friendly universe, not empirically but intuitively knowing all is well.

In our world of destruction and re-creation we seem to be in a constant state of chaos as we try to self organize our way to broader and deeper perceptions. It is all about creation, and chaos is what inspires creation, co-creating within the expanding consciousness of the universe. We are deeply connected to the universe, we are the universes, there is no separate or independent reality; we are the universe as the universe is us. It is through our imagination that the universe becomes aware of itself. The universe is nothing more than consciousness. Evolution is the evolution of consciousness. Infinity is a dream so therefore all that is and was is dreaming.

From our microcosmic perception within the greater cosmos it seems our tiny speck of existence is on the verge of self-destruction. Are we to become extinct as a physical biological organism, becoming no longer viable as a necessary or effective ingredient in the overall evolutionary unfolding of the universe, a mere victim of quantum probabilities? Do we really have any creative output against a predetermined universal will? Has the destructive path of the military industrial complex proven to be historically cyclically suppressing evolution, perhaps even to the point of regression? Or do we have a choice a free will to create our destiny and to have sway within an evolving integral universe?

We have a choice the free will to create our destiny.

Freedom and creation are one and the same the core essence of life. It is life. Without free will life would not exist. The big bang was nothing more than inspiration, an awesome manifestation of the creative free will materializing energy.

—

Although it may appear on the surface that we are just spinning our wheels heading nowhere except into an abyss of comic madness, but underlying our limited perception burns a sense of hope. This hope is found in the process of creation, sacrifice and resurrection.

The dynamic self-organizing universe is never static but always on the move, creating with the passion and intensity of Vincent Van Gogh. The title of the universe story is artistic energy not dead mechanical matter. The universes, is not a preset calibrated machine but alive and unpredictable. The whole is made up of parts and in turn that whole later becomes a part of a future whole. Metamorphous is the nature of all existence, and it's from this awareness that the emotional wisdom of hope survives. In the evolutionary process early cellular prokaryotes created eukaryotic cells, and we must give thanks to these cells for having created sex. These cells are literally our ancestors. Just as they transformed the very essence of their nature, we too, in the future, may transcend beyond the very essence of human nature. Perhaps we are merely a link, a stepping stone in the continual unpredictable evolutionary flow, where we will be metamorphosed into something absolutely amazing, beyond what our contemporary imagination can even begin to perceive. Perhaps this process is done out of a desire to survive or maybe just done out of pure joy of creation. We must all sacrifice equally together in order to insure the expansion of our evolutionary collective consciousness.

This evolutionary transformation may not only have an effect on our conscious awareness but may alter our physical features as well, in other words in the future human beings could evolve into entirely different forms, perhaps stripping off the veils, uncovering their inner divine essence. Perhaps all the inhabited planets throughout the whole universe are a collective unit of free consciousness evolving into a 'heaven on earth' type scenario, the solar consciousness experiment.

So even though history hasn't painted a very flattering picture of the human race all is not hopeless for it does not necessarily mean this pattern will continue, especially when you consider that humankind didn't really appear on the planet that long ago when compared to the age of the universe it evolved from. From that perspective one could infer that humankind is only in a stage of infancy, at least on planet earth, just getting ready to attempt its first step. This first step could be a transcendental step into mystical science, a dawning of a holistic, cosmological state of consciousness allowing us to enter into new forms of existence and purpose within the essence of being human.

Such prophetic insight has a high probability of unfolding especially now that scientific discovery has shown that nature may not be a dead machine that ultimately breaks down and stops working but a self organizing system that is fully alive and capable of organizing its continual survival. We have the capacity and the choice to create tomorrow even though today we may not know what it is we are about to create. That is the mystery of life, the ability to create but never really knowing for sure what it is you are about to create.

It's a mysterious, expanding universe, analogous to the mind expansion one experiences on LSD. Observations of exploding stars show that cosmic expansion may actually be accelerating due to an unknown, repulsive, divine energy. This is interesting in the context of accelerated cosmic expansion and the expansion of human self-awareness, the self-awareness that distinguishes humans from other life forms in our bio-system. And what is interesting is that cosmic acceleration seems to have begun at about the same time humankind and its nature of conscious self-reflection first appeared on the planet. I intuitively sense not a coincidence but a connection between cosmic expansion and human consciousness, an interconnected expansion unfolding as one.

We might be on the verge of shifting into higher realms of collective consciousness, becoming more unified as a whole being instead of separated individual entities as we have been directed and conditioned to be from the cultural pulpit of Cartesian philosophy. This shift may be activated by our individual instinct to survive, there by inspiring the creative will to evolve cooperatively for our present mode of conscious awareness falls short of what is needed to ignite the spark of universal will.

One can discern in evolution a repeating pattern in which aggressive competition leads to the threat of extinction, which is then avoided by the formation of cooperative alliances. Elisabet Sahtouris

In spite of the historical positive effects and enormous contribution of western material progress it's time for a change. Maybe if we look at the big picture this seeming chaos brought on by western civilization may be indirectly steering us back on path via the underlying subtleness of chaos theory, creating order out of disorder through our creative ability to self organize bringing us to peace and equality. In other words discoveries coming out of the age of enlightenment may have served humanity at some time in the past but they are no longer viable and to remain locked in that outdated mode of doing business will only destroy us. Einstein said " No problem can be solved from the same consciousness that created it," To continue into the future in a dualistic mechanistic frame of reference, exploiting the natural world for selfish illusive individual desires will only bring us more wars of mass destruction, environmental pollution, social inequality and separation.

It's appalling to be living in the 21st century and to be still riding off to war killing one another as if though we were still living in the times of the Roman Empire.

With each new sunrise the negative effects of a Cartesian perception of reality will become more and more noticeable to the masses. It will become no longer possible to be in denial of the harmful effects that our destroying our environment and this will sound off the alarm. And through this witnessing we may finally begin to assess the damages and make the necessary adjustments needed to insure our survival: sharing the natural resources with absolute equality along with sustainable living. Classical physics had put too much trust and reliance into the empirical, rational, logical understandings of the underlying workings of nature, analyzing and observing nature from the outside, objectively, in its efforts to control and manipulate, while completely ignoring the subjective side of our nature. But now is the time for change and modern science is setting a new course bringing us a new cultural language, a different way of thinking and understanding, an alternate perception of the meaning of reality going beyond the cultural confines of logic and common sense, erasing the line between the objective/subjective, spirituality/science. We have developed our objective left brain well enough while all the time ignoring our subjective right brain, now it's time begin to realize that the answers to our most pressing, puzzling problems may be found in the nonlinear patterns of right brain intuition.

So now we must continue to put more emphasis and effort into researching our emotional inner-selves, giving credibility to our emotional feelings, intuition, psychic phenomena and creative imaginations as we enter deep into the abyss of the irrational, illogical, nonlinear modes of being; where the creative spirit will be liberated from the limiting bounds of our left brain perceptions, spawning higher states of conscious awareness. We will begin to question our ethics and human values inherent in our institutions of culture that seem to be structured for the sole purpose of controlling and manipulating matter and energy only to benefit a selective segment of the global population. We need to apply the informational wisdom coming out of the new science to simply learn how to live in harmony with one another as well as the natural environment. We will be able to build a decentralized global community on cultural values that brings meaning and purpose to the human experience. This will have a positive effect in ending poverty, social injustice, human rights abuses, environmental pollution and wars of mass destruction.

"The lack of advances in the understanding of human behavior and inner experience prevented any development of our ability to...stop the poisoning of our planet, or to prevent wars. As one of us has shown elsewhere, there has been no advance in the understanding of the causes of war since Hellenistic times." Lawrence Lesham &Henry

Margenau.

Discoveries in science are taking us deeper and deeper into the realms of the invisible, the non-physical. Quantum physics is telling us that there is no substance to physical reality and that matter is created through the interaction of energy fields. Our consciousness is an energy field so by its very nature it can interact with other quantum energy fields participating in the temporal creation of form and function. If this is so then we are not observers but participators in an unfolding, creative universe, so therefore anything is possible. Through the thoughts within our imagination we can create anything we want, such a psychic phenomenon gives us unlimited possibilities. So therefore we are not bound by the chains of the cultural status quo and all its negative side effects of war, violence and children dying from hunger, we no longer have to live by the slogan 'that just the way it is' because now we know through our imagination we can manifest whatever we want.

"When science begins the study of non-physical phenomena, it will make more progress in one decade than in all the centuries of existence". Nikola Tesla.

The nonsensical foundation found in the quantum world allows us to question our logical, rational perception of what constitutes reality. Through this new awareness we may now begin to question the status quo and ask the hard question, is the status quo really serving us, even the ones who seem to be benefiting from it the most? Would everyone in the world be happier if we were equally sharing the natural resources, including the rich?

It is from this quantum vision that we begin to re-create and evolve with a fresh sense of wonder into a mysterious universe. It's from this foundation where we will begin to develop our right brain characteristics, the feminine and the receptive. By doing this we can hopefully in the future increase our capacity for human compassion and acceptance, evolving into a state of consciousness that propagates holistic love. Through exploring our subjective nature, the depths of our interior, we will be collectively led to a natural mystical experience beyond the constraining boundaries of dogmatic religiosity and spiritual cosmetics to places never before imagined.

So science has now come to realize how everything within the universe is interconnected, how our consciousness is deeply embedded, floating and splashing in an universal quantum pool, revealing even if only one person is starving it affects are omnipresent.

By becoming more intelligible and aware of this interconnectedness we will begin to see ourselves in each other as well as all of nature. The positive consequences of this blossoming self-realization will make us less inclined to exploit the natural environment or harm each other by realizing that in harming others we our only harming ourselves. We will begin to treat each other with more understanding, kindness, and empathy. There by igniting the compassion within us, giving us the will needed to bring justice, equality and peace to our planet. This awareness is already showing signs of permeating into our world through grassroots community organizing, indigenous people all over the world are coming together making their voices heard, demanding economic equality, human rights, justice, and putting a stop to the environmental destruction that is destroying their land and water.

The scientific concept of an all-pervading unity, the inter-relation of all things and events is connecting mysticism with modern science. Science and spirituality are evolving into a unity of oneness. Such a merger could possibly mean the dawning of a collective shift in conscious awareness permeating multiple dimensions of divinity, changing our perceptions of everyday physical reality. Such a suggestion gives credibility to the intuitive self as well as the validity of direct divine experiences and visions emanating from within. The connection between ancient mystical wisdom and modern physics is taking us on a journey. The prophetic insights coming out of all ancient wisdom traditions tells us we are in the midst of a new spiritual transformation in consciousness. The coming together of ancient wisdom and modern physics will have an unprecedented effect on our spiritual evolution.

{Jesus said: When you make the two into one, you will be called the sons of men. When you say," Move

Mountain!" it will move.} Nothing will be impossible in a unified world. There are no limitations or boundaries to the imagination; all desires are there to be fulfilled. Just imagination it and it will happen.

—

The seed of evolution is the continual resistance to outdated consciousness. The status quo signifies stagnation an uninspired consciousness becoming separated from the dynamic creative fires of divinity, where the soul of evolution gravitates towards love. It has always been the radical voice of the prophet as artist resisting the conforming consciousness of the status quo who fuels the blaze of evolution manifesting human consciousness into collective unity. Artist William Blake was one such prophet, who, with compelling passion, spoke vehemently against the status quo. Blake had envisioned a future of 'heaven on earth', a New Jerusalem of unity within diversity. He saw the ruling elite, the status quo of both church and state as a major factor in suppressing his vision. And felt it was the duty of the artist (as prophet) to uncover the truth. Blake felt that the church and state were too comfortable with the material, industrial, and mechanistic ways of the world, and in wanting to preserve that comfort they would have to suppress the voice of the prophet. The voice of the prophet was suppressed by devaluing the irrational, mystical, psychic, visionary side of our nature. The exercise of the imagination was placed into the subtext of lunacy. For

Blake complete freedom and liberty were necessary ingredients for people to actualize their inner visions and the institutions of state suppressed this spiritual self-realization.

Thus it is the radical voice of the prophet/artist who turns the wheels of evolution forward towards the truth of our divine nature. But now we have the voice of the scientist merging with the voice of the mystic/artist bringing to our awareness that humanity is intimately integrated with the evolution of the cosmos, which ultimately means the expansion of consciousness. This is a sign of great hope that humanity will finally become united within itself and with the earth that nourishes and feeds us.

Evolving from an analytical, mechanistic nature to a creative, intuitive, holistic one signifies a spiritual transformation. Being spiritual in this space does not mean being more religious but being more sensitive and compassionate. It is a state of being that is sensual, intuitive, creative, dreamy, imaginative and interdependent. It is the existential void, where non-physical, ethereal energy hides itself from human power. I think I heard the Dali Lama say something like we don't need more Buddhist we need more compassionate people.

Yes it seems our current economic, political structure is at odds with this cosmological spiritual transformation. For instance capitalism breeds off the dualistic concept of competition and the anthropocentric manipulation and exploitation of nature. Again the problem with this is humankind being nature ends up inadvertently manipulating and exploiting its self. As we shift into higher dimensions of consciousness our political, economic infrastructure will shift as well, effortlessly, without violence or dissent. This shift will naturally occur as we lose the desire for consuming non-essential commodities, thus making a profit driven capitalistic economy obsolete. Our desire for material wealth and the ego gratification it brings will be replaced by the desire to inner-connect with one another and the natural environment from within a space of deep intimacy and inspired energy. Our energy and focus will not be directed towards commerce instead we will all begin to create art in all its various shapes, forms and functions as community workers. As we develop and increase the use of our intuitive, receptive, right brain characteristics we will begin to create new forms of human fulfillment never before imagined thus relieving us from the culturally conditioned vices of consumerism, static boredom and all the negative side effects it has had on our ecosystem. As Blake contemplates "For every pleasure money is useless".

We are entering into a new era of interconnectedness and cooperation, leaving behind the illusive perception of separation and fear, conquer and divide. The old school vanguard administering the power politics of greed, deceit, control and domination has run its course. Within the social construct of this new perception we will begin to see the dire need to work on our relations within the eco-community living in sustainable harmony with all of creation to insure our survival on earth and to stay connected to the earth and its evolutionary purpose. We are now living in a crucial time of cosmological evolution, a quantum surprise giving birth to an unprecedented collective earth consciousness, which will bring about the peace, justice and equality we have all for eon's been so eagerly awaiting.

{Jesus said: when you were one, you became two. When you became two, what will you do?]

Share-Sustain -Survive.